THE PSYCHOLOGY OF SPENDING

"Master Your Money Habits and Avoid Financial Traps" - What, Why, When, & How You Should Buy –

S S Dhar

[The Psychology of Spending]

ISBN: 978-93-343-4021-1

Publisher – S S Dhar

Publisher Website - www.ssdhar.com

Author – S S Dhar

Legal Notice:

Disclaimer Notice:

Please note the information contained within this document is for educational and entertainment purpose only every attempt has been made to provide accurate, up to date and reliable complete information. No warranties of any kind are expressed or implied. Please consult a licensed professional before attempting any techniques outlined in this book.

By reading this document, the reader agrees that under no circumstances are is the author responsible for any losses, direct or indirect, which are incurred as a result of the use of information contained within this document, including, but not limited to, --errors, omissions, or inaccuracies (something may be estimated).

DEDICATION

This book is dedicated to anyone seeking to break free from the cycle of mindless spending and financial uncertainty. It is for those who are ready to take control of their money and make mindful decisions that align with their long-term goals. May this journey lead you to a life of intentional spending, financial peace, and true wealth—not just in material possessions, but in freedom and security.

I also dedicate this work to my family and friends, whose constant encouragement, love, and belief in me have been my pillars of strength throughout this process. Without your support, this book would not have been possible.

Finally, to all the readers who are ready to change their financial future—your willingness to learn and grow will shape your path to lasting prosperity. May you gain the clarity and confidence to master your money habits and avoid the traps that stand in your way.

THE PSYCHOLOGY OF SPENDING

MASTER YOUR MONEY HABITS
&
AVOID FINANCIAL TRAPS

Preface

Money, an inescapable force in our daily lives, is not just a tool for buying goods and services. It is also a source of psychological significance that shapes much of our behavior, relationships, and sense of self-worth. We live in a world where consumerism defines a large part of our identities, yet most of us have never taken the time to reflect deeply on why we spend the way we do. Spending money has become so routine for many that it operates almost on autopilot, driven by unconscious motives, emotional triggers, and societal pressures.

This book, ***The Psychology of Spending: What, Why, When & How You Should Buy – Master Your Money Habits and Avoid Financial Traps***, aims to peel back the layers of the psychological forces that influence our spending habits. The goal is to offer readers a comprehensive understanding of why we buy, how we make financial decisions, and how to cultivate healthier, more intentional spending behaviors. From the psychological drivers behind our impulse buys to the cultural pressures that shape our attitudes toward money, this book will help you unravel the hidden factors at play when it comes to your finances.

The Complexity of Spending: More Than Just Money

At first glance, spending might seem like a simple exchange: you give money in exchange for a product or service. However, the psychology behind spending is anything but simple. Money is tied to emotions, status, identity, and even our self-worth. The act of purchasing something can be a moment of joy, a way to relieve stress, a method of social comparison, or an attempt to fill an emotional void. We often buy things not because we truly need them, but because of how they make us feel in the moment.

Every time we reach for our wallets or swipe our cards, we're making a choice. But what guides those choices? What is the psychological impulse behind our purchases? Why do we frequently spend without considering the consequences? What do our buying habits say about us as individuals and as a society?

These are some of the questions this book seeks to answer. We will delve into the psychological mechanisms that drive consumer behavior, unpacking the emotional and cognitive biases that often lead to spending decisions that do not align with our long-term financial goals. Whether we are trying to fill an emotional need, keep up with social pressures, or simply experience the fleeting joy of acquiring something new, there is always more beneath the surface of a purchase than meets the eye.

Understanding the Forces Behind Our Spending

A significant portion of our spending habits is influenced by the emotional triggers and cognitive biases that shape our decision-making processes. These include:

- **Instant Gratification**: The desire for immediate satisfaction drives much of our spending behavior. Whether it's indulging in a luxury purchase or buying a small treat to soothe stress, the pursuit of instant pleasure often trumps rational decision-making.

- **Emotional Spending**: Many people use spending as a coping mechanism for negative emotions such as anxiety, sadness, or boredom. Shopping offers a temporary sense of relief, but it rarely addresses the root causes of emotional distress, leading to a cycle of emotional spending that becomes habitual and financially damaging.

- **Social Influence**: In our interconnected, social media-driven world, we are constantly exposed to the lifestyles, products, and experiences of others. The desire to keep up with friends, family, and influencers can lead to impulsive purchasing decisions that are rooted in social comparison and the fear of missing out (FOMO).

- **Cultural and Societal Expectations**: From the brands we wear to the vacations we take, cultural norms and societal pressures play a massive role in shaping our spending behavior. Advertisers and marketers know how to leverage these societal values to sell products that promise to fulfill a particular ideal or lifestyle.

Through this book, we aim to uncover these psychological factors and explore how they work in harmony (and sometimes against our best interests) to influence our spending decisions. But understanding these forces is only the first step; the ultimate goal is to empower you to break free from unhealthy financial behaviors and develop a mindset that allows you to make smarter, more intentional decisions about your money.

The Consequences of Mindless Spending

At the heart of *The Psychology of Spending* lies a fundamental question: *How much of our spending is conscious, and how much is driven by unconscious motivations?* While occasional indulgence isn't inherently problematic, habitual mindless spending can have serious long-term consequences. The impulse to buy for emotional reasons, the lure of "limited-time" sales, or the pressure to project a certain image can lead to financial strain, debt, and a lack of savings.

If you find yourself living paycheck to paycheck, constantly making impulse purchases, or unable to save for your future, it's time to take a hard look at the psychology behind your spending. By understanding the emotions and biases that drive your financial decisions, you can begin to shift your spending habits, build healthier financial routines, and regain control over your money.

The ability to delay gratification, resist impulse buying, and make thoughtful purchasing decisions is not only important for financial health but also for emotional well-being. Reducing unnecessary spending can lower stress, improve financial security, and provide the emotional satisfaction of knowing you are making decisions that align with your long-term goals.

This book isn't about making you feel guilty for spending; it's about helping you gain awareness of why you spend and how to shift your mindset to one that is more focused on mindful, intentional purchases. We'll explore various strategies to help you make better financial choices and overcome the psychological barriers that lead to poor spending habits.

Breaking Free from Financial Traps

One of the primary goals of this book is to help you avoid the financial traps that many people fall into without even realizing it. These traps often involve spending that is driven by fear, impulse, social pressure, or misguided expectations, leaving individuals with little savings, unnecessary debt, or a diminished sense of financial freedom.

Common financial traps include:

- **The Debt Trap**: Accumulating debt due to impulse buying, credit card use, and living beyond your means.
- **The FOMO Trap**: The fear of missing out on experiences, trends, or social validation that leads to overspending and social comparison.
- **The Instant Gratification Trap**: The desire for immediate pleasure and the purchase of things we don't need, which only provides short-term satisfaction at the cost of long-term financial stability.

Through this book, we'll show you how to recognize these traps in your own life and how to implement strategies for avoiding them. We'll also dive into practical ways to break free from the habits that may be holding you back and start building healthier financial behaviors. From the psychology of how we're conditioned by advertisers to the habits we form from childhood, we will examine the root causes of financial struggles and provide actionable steps to help you change your relationship with money.

Empowering You to Take Control of Your Spending

The ultimate goal of *The Psychology of Spending* is to empower you to take control of your financial future. By understanding the psychological forces that influence your spending behavior, you can begin to make more intentional decisions that align with your values and long-term goals. Whether it's developing a deeper sense of self-awareness, learning to practice delayed gratification, or setting clear financial goals, this book provides you with the tools and knowledge to break free from unhealthy financial patterns.

By understanding the emotions and subconscious drivers that influence our spending habits, we can make decisions that not only benefit our financial health but also promote greater emotional well-being. After all, money is not just about numbers—it's about the choices we make and the way those choices reflect our values and priorities.

How This Book Can Help You

This book is designed to help you recognize and understand the psychological forces at play when it comes to spending, and to provide you with the tools to make conscious, intentional decisions about money. Here's what you can expect to learn from each chapter:

- **The Roots of Spending Behavior**: Discover how your early life experiences, cultural conditioning, and subconscious triggers shape the way you spend money.

- **The Impact of Social Influence**: Learn how peer pressure, social media, and cultural norms influence your spending decisions, and how to break free from unhealthy comparisons.

- **The Psychology of Instant Gratification**: Understand the powerful pull of immediate rewards and how to practice delayed gratification for long-term financial success.

- **The Power of Marketing and Advertising**: Uncover the psychological techniques that marketers use to influence your spending and how to resist the urge to buy based on emotional triggers.

- **Emotional Spending and Coping Mechanisms**: Explore how emotions drive spending and how to develop healthier coping mechanisms that don't rely on retail therapy.

- **The Delayed Gratification Approach**: Learn how to practice patience and self-discipline to make smarter, more intentional financial decisions.

- **Proven Strategies for Saving Money**: Discover practical strategies to save more money, from budgeting to cutting unnecessary expenses, and how to start building your financial security.

- **Overcoming Financial Traps**: Identify common financial traps and how to avoid them, empowering you to take control of your money and avoid unnecessary debt.

A Final Thought

Money doesn't have to be a source of anxiety, confusion, or regret. With awareness and knowledge, you can develop a healthier, more intentional relationship with money. This book is not just about managing money—it's about understanding the psychology behind why we spend, and how we can leverage that knowledge to make better, more fulfilling financial decisions.

As you begin your journey toward mastering your money habits, remember: **The key to financial well-being is not about how much you earn, but how you spend and save.** Through the insights and strategies in this book, you'll be equipped to make choices that align with your true values, helping you achieve financial peace and freedom.

Let's begin this journey of self-awareness, empowerment, and transformation.

Table of Contents

Introduction: Understanding Your Money Habits

Money is more than just a tool for exchanging goods and services. It's a powerful force that shapes our lives, influences our decisions, and affects our relationships. Despite its central role in everyday life, many people rarely stop to reflect on their financial behaviors or ask the fundamental question: *Why do I spend the way I do?*

The truth is, the way we manage, spend, and save money is deeply influenced by psychological factors—emotions, beliefs, values, past experiences, and even the culture we are immersed in. From impulsive purchases to careful, well-thought-out investments, the act of spending is often driven by forces we don't even realize. The psychology of spending is a complex interplay of these various factors that, when left unchecked, can lead us into financial traps that are hard to escape.

In this book, we will explore the many dimensions of how and why people spend. We will look at the deep psychological forces at play when we pull out our wallets, and how those forces often lead us to make financial choices that may not align with our long-term goals. Our primary aim is to unravel these factors, providing you with the tools and knowledge needed to change your money habits and take back control of your financial future.

The Power of Your Money Habits

Before we dive into the psychology of spending, it's important to first understand the power of your money habits. Whether you realize it or not, your financial behavior is a product of years of conditioning. From childhood lessons about money to the messages you absorb through advertisements, the media, and your social circles, your relationship with money is shaped by many influences.

Money habits are formed over time, often through experiences that become ingrained in your psyche. Think about how you feel when you make a purchase. Do you experience a rush of happiness or relief? Or do you feel guilt or anxiety, especially when it comes to larger, more significant purchases? These emotional reactions can have a major impact on your spending choices. Many people make purchases based on how they feel in the moment, rather than on practical considerations like necessity or budget. This leads to what is often referred to as "emotional spending," where people buy things to make themselves feel better, even if it means going beyond their means.

The connection between emotions and money is powerful. In fact, our feelings and subconscious desires often override our logical decision-making processes. For instance, you might know that you don't need another pair of shoes or that you're over your budget, but something inside of you convinces you to buy anyway. This is the psychology of spending at work—compelling us to act against our better judgment.

The Impact of External Factors

In addition to our emotional responses, external factors such as marketing, social pressures, and cultural expectations play a massive role in shaping our spending habits. Every day, we are bombarded with advertisements, many of which appeal to our desires for status, belonging, or approval. The idea of having the "latest" gadgets, the most stylish clothes, or the trendiest car often becomes more than a simple desire; it becomes a need that we feel compelled to fulfill.

Marketing plays on these psychological triggers, offering us instant gratification in exchange for our money. Limited-time offers, discounts, and flashy advertisements are just a few of the ways companies push us to make purchases we don't necessarily need. Advertisers know the power of human psychology, and they know how to make us feel that we cannot live without their products. This is why we're often persuaded to buy things on impulse, ignoring our own financial goals in the process.

The Psychology of Instant Gratification

One of the strongest forces driving our spending behavior is the desire for instant gratification. From the moment we get a paycheck to the moment we're faced with a sale, the craving for immediate pleasure or satisfaction is overwhelming. It's much easier to buy something that promises quick joy rather than wait and save for something we truly need or desire.

Instant gratification is the psychological tendency to favor immediate rewards over long-term benefits. In the context of spending, this could mean purchasing an item because it feels good in the moment—whether it's a luxury item, an impulse buy, or simply a convenience purchase. But the long-term consequences of this behavior often go unnoticed in the heat of the moment.

This constant pursuit of immediate pleasure has detrimental effects on our finances. The more we give in to the impulse of buying things that satisfy short-term desires, the more we neglect the long-term consequences, like debt accumulation, financial instability, and delayed financial goals. The challenge, then, is not to eliminate all forms of spending, but to develop the ability to delay gratification and make purchasing decisions that align with your long-term financial well-being.

How Emotional Triggers Lead to Financial Traps

Emotional spending is one of the most pervasive behaviors in personal finance. It refers to the tendency to spend money based on emotions–such as boredom, stress, or sadness–rather than necessity. Emotional spending can create a cycle where you feel better temporarily after making a purchase, but the relief is short-lived, and the financial consequences remain. For example, you may feel a temporary rush of happiness after buying something on impulse, but later experience regret or guilt.

These emotional triggers lead many people to fall into financial traps, such as running up credit card debt or depleting their savings on things they don't really need. Emotional spending is often fueled by the belief that buying something new will bring happiness or ease emotional pain. This, however, is a temporary fix that only serves to worsen your financial situation in the long run.

Understanding the psychology behind emotional spending is essential for breaking free from this cycle. The goal isn't to eliminate emotions from spending but to develop greater awareness of how your emotions influence your purchasing decisions. By identifying these triggers, you can learn to control them and make more rational, purposeful financial choices.

The Goal of This Book: Master Your Money Habits

The purpose of this book is to help you understand the underlying psychological factors that influence your spending, so you can make smarter, more intentional decisions with your money. By mastering your money habits, you can avoid the financial traps that many people fall into and set yourself up for long-term financial success.

In the chapters that follow, we will explore key concepts such as the psychology of social influence, the impact of marketing, and the role of fear and scarcity in decision-making. You will also learn about emotional spending, habitual purchases, and how to reframe your thinking to develop healthier money habits.

Ultimately, this book will empower you to recognize the mental and emotional barriers that prevent you from saving money, and provide you with strategies to overcome them. You will gain valuable insights into how to prioritize long-term financial goals over short-term desires, and how to build a mindset that supports sustainable financial habits.

Conclusion: Moving Toward Financial Freedom

Money is more than just numbers in a bank account–it's an emotional and psychological experience that influences every aspect of our lives. By taking control of your spending habits, you're not just changing the way you manage money; you're changing the way you think about it. Financial freedom doesn't come from avoiding all spending, but from understanding your financial behavior and aligning it with your goals and values.

As you move forward in your financial journey, remember that awareness is the first step to change. By the end of this book, you'll have a deeper understanding of your spending patterns, a toolkit for mastering your money habits, and the confidence to avoid the financial traps that hold you back.

Chapter 1: The Roots of Spending Behavior

Spending behavior is a deeply ingrained part of who we are. From the smallest impulse purchase to the most calculated investments, the way we spend our money is influenced by a complex mix of psychological, emotional, social, and environmental factors. In this chapter, we will explore the root causes of spending behavior, looking at how early life experiences, cultural conditioning, and subconscious triggers shape our financial decisions. By understanding the roots of spending behavior, we can begin to unravel why we make certain choices with our money, and more importantly, how we can start making better, more mindful decisions in the future.

Early Life Experiences and Their Influence on Money

One of the first places where our spending behavior is shaped is in childhood. The environment we grow up in has a significant impact on how we view money and its role in our lives. Think about how your parents or guardians managed money. Were they cautious and conservative with their spending? Or did they splurge without much thought? Did they talk about money openly or keep it a secret? These early experiences set the tone for how we approach money as adults.

For example, children who grow up in families that struggle financially might develop a scarcity mindset. They may grow up thinking that money is hard to come by and that they must hold onto it tightly. This could lead to a fear of spending, even when it's necessary, as they may feel that there won't be enough to go around. On the other hand, children who grow up in more affluent households might develop a sense of entitlement or an overspending tendency, as they associate money with comfort and security.

Even if your parents didn't explicitly teach you about money, their behaviors likely left a lasting imprint on you. Did they make purchasing decisions based on emotion, such as buying something as a way to cope with stress? If so, you might develop a similar approach to spending, where you buy things to elevate your mood or deal with difficult emotions.

Cultural and Societal Conditioning

The culture we live in also plays a major role in shaping our spending behavior. From an early age, we are bombarded with messages about what we "should" have, do, and experience in life. Media, advertisements, and even our social circles constantly shape our idea of what is normal and acceptable when it comes to spending. These influences can create powerful societal pressures that lead us to spend in ways we might not have considered otherwise.

Consider the societal expectations placed on us when it comes to material possessions. The need to keep up with the latest trends in technology, fashion, or lifestyle is ever-present. This constant pressure to conform can push us into overspending, especially if we feel like we'll be left behind if we don't meet these external standards. Our identity becomes tied to the things we own, and in some cases, we are conditioned to believe that happiness and status are defined by what we can buy.

Advertising plays a huge role in this societal conditioning. Every day, we're exposed to hundreds, if not thousands, of advertisements that promise to make our lives better if we simply buy a particular product or service. These ads don't just sell products; they sell an image—a lifestyle or an ideal that we're supposed to strive for. Whether it's the latest smartphone, a designer handbag, or a luxury car, the message is clear: purchasing these items will somehow make our lives more fulfilling.

But the question is, do these material possessions really bring lasting happiness, or are we simply falling prey to marketing tactics that exploit our desires? The root of this behavior lies in the subconscious belief that owning things equals happiness. It's a dangerous cycle because once we start spending to satisfy emotional needs, we risk becoming trapped in a never-ending pursuit of more.

Psychological Factors: Emotions and Impulse

One of the most powerful drivers of spending behavior is emotion. It's common for people to make purchases based on how they feel in the moment. Whether it's buying a new outfit to cheer up after a stressful day, grabbing an expensive coffee to feel more energized, or treating ourselves to a night out because we've had a tough week, emotional triggers are often the catalyst for spending.

Emotions like stress, anxiety, and boredom can lead to what's known as "emotional spending." This happens when people use shopping as a way to cope with negative feelings. For example, someone might buy something they don't need or can't afford as a way to temporarily escape from stress or sadness. The act of purchasing something new provides a fleeting sense of relief, but it often doesn't address the underlying emotional issue. In fact, emotional spending can lead to more problems, such as buyer's remorse or financial strain, which then trigger more emotional spending as a form of self-soothing.

This emotional cycle is reinforced by the brain's reward system. When we make a purchase, especially one that makes us feel good, our brain releases dopamine, the "feel-good" chemical. This provides instant gratification, creating a positive association between spending and pleasure. Unfortunately, this quick fix can become addictive. Over time, we may begin to seek out shopping or spending as a way to satisfy emotional needs, leading to overspending and, in some cases, debt accumulation.

The Power of Immediate Gratification

In today's world, we are constantly surrounded by opportunities for instant gratification. With the click of a button, we can order products online, make impulsive purchases, or sign up for subscription services that promise quick rewards. The rise of e-commerce and subscription-based models has made it easier than ever to indulge in instant gratification.

The psychology behind this behavior is rooted in what's known as "impulse buying." Impulse buying occurs when a person makes a spontaneous purchase without giving it much thought or considering the long-term consequences. Often, the desire to buy something is driven by a momentary feeling or temptation. For example, seeing a product on sale might spark a desire to buy it, even if it's not something we need or were planning to purchase.

The lure of instant gratification can be a powerful force, especially in a society that constantly reinforces the need for immediate rewards. But this tendency to prioritize short-term pleasure over long-term goals is what gets many people into financial trouble. We often forget about the bigger picture—saving for the future, paying off debt, or investing in our long-term well-being—because we are too focused on the pleasure of buying something in the moment.

The Role of Cognitive Biases in Spending Decisions

Cognitive biases also play a significant role in our spending habits. These are systematic patterns of deviation from rational thinking that often influence our decisions without us even realizing it. For example, the "anchoring bias" occurs when we base our purchasing decisions on the first piece of information we see—such as a sale price or a recommended retail price. If an item is marked down from $200 to $100, we might think we're getting a great deal, even if the item isn't something we actually need.

Similarly, the "scarcity effect" makes us value things more when they seem limited in supply. The mere idea that a product is in short supply or that a sale is ending soon can trigger a fear of missing out (FOMO), leading us to make hasty purchases. This bias plays into the hands of marketers, who often use phrases like "limited-time offer" or "only a few left" to encourage people to buy quickly.

Another bias is the "status quo bias," which leads us to stick with the way we've always done things. For example, if we've always purchased certain items from a specific store or brand, we might continue to do so even if it's no longer the best option financially. This bias often prevents us from making smarter, more cost-effective choices.

Breaking Free from the Roots of Spending Behavior

The key to overcoming the negative aspects of our spending behavior lies in awareness. Once we understand how our early life experiences, cultural conditioning, emotions, and cognitive biases influence our decisions, we can begin to break free from the patterns that no longer serve us. The process of understanding and changing your spending behavior is a journey that requires self-reflection, discipline, and a willingness to challenge long-held beliefs about money.

In this book, we will provide strategies for recognizing and addressing these psychological and emotional triggers. By becoming more aware of the roots of our spending behavior, we can take control of our financial decisions and make choices that align with our true needs and long-term goals.

Chapter 2: The Impact of Social Influence

When it comes to spending, we often like to think of ourselves as independent decision-makers, guided solely by personal preference, logic, and necessity. However, in reality, our spending behavior is heavily influenced by the people around us, the culture we're immersed in, and the social norms that dictate what is considered "acceptable" or "desirable." This chapter explores the profound impact that social influence has on our spending habits, from the immediate effects of peer pressure to the more subtle ways in which advertising and societal expectations shape our desires and purchasing decisions.

Peer Pressure and Social Comparison

Humans are inherently social creatures, and our need for social acceptance often drives many of our decisions, including how we spend money. Peer pressure is a well-documented psychological phenomenon that affects individuals of all ages, and it plays a significant role in consumer behavior. Whether it's friends, family, or even colleagues, the people around us can exert considerable influence over our financial choices.

Peer pressure doesn't just apply to teenagers or young adults. It's a universal force that affects everyone. Adults, especially those in social or professional circles, often feel compelled to conform to the spending patterns of those around them. This is especially true in environments where social status is tied to material possessions. If a friend buys a new car, a luxury watch, or a designer handbag, it can trigger the desire to keep up with them, even if doing so stretches our finances.

Social comparison is another key factor in this dynamic. Social comparison theory, first proposed by psychologist Leon Festinger, suggests that we evaluate ourselves in relation to others. When it comes to spending, we often compare ourselves to those who seem to have more wealth or status. This comparison can create a sense of inadequacy, leading us to spend beyond our means in an attempt to "keep up" or "fit in." The desire to match the lifestyle of others, even when it's not financially viable, can lead to unnecessary purchases and financial stress.

Social Media and the "Insta-Effect"

In today's digital age, social media has become a powerful tool for influencing spending behavior. Platforms like Instagram, Facebook, Twitter, and Pinterest are filled with images of people showcasing their lives, including their most recent purchases, vacations, and experiences. The curated nature of these platforms creates a world where it often seems like everyone is living a more glamorous, more stylish, or more adventurous life than we are.

This phenomenon, often referred to as "Instagram envy" or "Facebook depression," can have a profound impact on our spending habits. Studies have shown that constant exposure to the carefully curated lives of others can lead to feelings of inadequacy or jealousy, prompting individuals to make purchases as a way to feel better about themselves or to "keep up." For example, seeing friends post about their luxurious vacations might lead someone to impulsively book a similar trip, even if it's beyond their budget, in an attempt to match the lifestyle they see online.

Social media influencers, who are paid to promote products, further perpetuate this cycle. Their recommendations, paired with polished images and engaging content, create a sense of trust and credibility that drives followers to purchase the items they endorse. These influencers often become "tastemakers," shaping the buying habits of their audience. The pressure to emulate the lifestyles of influencers, celebrities, or even friends on social media can drive people to make financial decisions that don't align with their personal goals or circumstances.

The Power of FOMO (Fear of Missing Out)

The fear of missing out, or FOMO, is a powerful social influence that drives many people to make purchases they don't really need. It's the emotional pull that arises when we perceive that others are experiencing something that we are not. Whether it's a limited-time offer, an exclusive event, or a trending product, FOMO triggers a sense of urgency that compels us to act quickly, even if it's not in our best interest.

FOMO is frequently used in marketing and advertising to encourage consumers to make impulsive decisions. Limited-time offers, flash sales, and "while supplies last" messaging all tap into this fear. The idea that something might be gone forever if we don't act fast creates a sense of urgency that often overrides our rational thinking. As a result, many people make purchases based on the fear of missing out, rather than on the actual value or need for the product.

FOMO is particularly potent in the context of social groups. If everyone in your circle is talking about a new product or a popular event, there's a natural desire to join in and not feel left out. This pressure to conform can lead to unplanned spending, as we buy into trends or products that we may not even have considered if left to our own devices.

Cultural Expectations and the Desire for Status

Beyond peer pressure and social media, cultural expectations and societal norms also have a significant impact on how we spend money. Different cultures have varying attitudes toward wealth, success, and material possessions. In some cultures, showing off one's wealth or possessions is seen as a sign of success, while in others, modesty and frugality are valued.

In cultures where wealth and status are highly valued, there is often an implicit pressure to display one's financial success through material possessions. This can manifest in the desire for a bigger house, a luxury car, or designer clothing, all of which signal a certain level of success. The desire for status is deeply ingrained in our social DNA, and many of us make purchases not because we need the item, but because it serves as a status symbol that elevates our perceived social standing.

For example, owning a high-end brand like Gucci or Louis Vuitton may not be necessary from a functional standpoint, but it can serve as a way to signal wealth and sophistication to others. This type of status-driven spending is not just about personal preference—it's often about societal expectations and the pressure to conform to a specific image of success.

The Impact of Groupthink on Spending

Groupthink is another social phenomenon that can influence spending behavior. It occurs when individuals in a group make decisions based on consensus or the desire to avoid conflict, rather than on independent thinking or rational analysis. In the context of spending, groupthink can occur in social situations where everyone is making similar purchasing decisions, such as a group vacation, a collective investment, or a joint purchase.

When people are part of a group that is collectively spending, there's a tendency to follow the crowd, even if it doesn't make financial sense. For example, a group of friends might decide to go on an expensive trip, and even though one person can't really afford it, they might go along with the group to avoid feeling left out. In these situations, people often make purchasing decisions based on the desire to belong, rather than on their own financial needs or goals.

Groupthink can also be influenced by social proof, another psychological concept that plays into our spending behavior. Social proof refers to the tendency to look to others for guidance in uncertain situations. If everyone around us is buying something, we assume it must be worthwhile or valuable. This is why trends and fads often spread so quickly—people are more likely to buy into something if they see that others are doing the same.

Overcoming Social Influence in Spending

While social influence is a powerful force, it's important to remember that we have control over our own spending decisions. By becoming aware of the social forces at play, we can make more conscious choices that align with our financial goals.

One way to reduce the impact of social influence on spending is to practice mindful consumption. This involves taking a step back before making a purchase and asking yourself whether the item aligns with your values and long-term goals, or whether it's simply a response to social pressure. Learning to say "no" to things that aren't truly necessary can help break the cycle of impulse spending.

Another strategy is to surround yourself with people who share your financial values. If you're part of a group that encourages overspending or keeping up with the Joneses, it may be time to find a new social circle that prioritizes financial independence, saving, and investing. Having a supportive network that encourages responsible spending can make it easier to resist the pressure to overspend.

Finally, learning to embrace your own values and defining success on your own terms—rather than according to societal expectations—can help you break free from the cycle of materialism and status-driven spending.

Conclusion: Social Influence Is Everywhere, But It Doesn't Have to Control You

Social influence is an inescapable part of the human experience. From peer pressure to the allure of social media and the desire for status, external forces shape our spending habits in ways we may not fully realize. However, by understanding these influences, we can take steps to make more mindful, intentional spending decisions.

Chapter 3: The Psychology of Instant Gratification

In today's fast-paced world, the desire for immediate satisfaction has become a central driving force behind many of our decisions—particularly when it comes to spending money. The act of buying something gives us a brief moment of pleasure, an instant rush that momentarily relieves the tension of wanting something, whether it's a new gadget, a fashion trend, or an experience. This chapter delves deep into the psychology of instant gratification, exploring how it affects our spending behavior, the consequences of chasing short-term pleasure, and practical strategies to overcome this impulse for the sake of long-term financial well-being.

What is Instant Gratification?

Instant gratification refers to the desire to experience pleasure or fulfillment without delay. It's the urge to have something now, rather than waiting for a more optimal or lasting reward. This psychological craving for immediate reward is deeply rooted in our biology, influenced by the brain's reward system. When we purchase something, eat something delicious, or receive something we want, our brain releases dopamine—the chemical associated with pleasure and reward.

In the context of spending, instant gratification manifests as the impulse to buy something in the moment because it feels good, rather than carefully evaluating whether the purchase is truly necessary. For instance, you may find yourself buying the latest tech gadget just because it promises a quick boost in satisfaction, even though your current phone is still functional and meets all your needs.

While experiencing satisfaction in the moment feels rewarding, it often overlooks the long-term consequences–both financial and psychological–that may arise later. Instant gratification creates a cycle of impulsive spending that can leave us with buyer's remorse, debt, or a lack of funds to achieve long-term goals like saving for retirement or purchasing a home.

The Biological and Psychological Drivers of Instant Gratification

Instant gratification is not a modern phenomenon; it's part of our evolutionary wiring. Our ancestors needed quick rewards to stay motivated to perform essential tasks such as hunting and gathering. The need for immediate rewards was directly tied to survival–getting food, shelter, or safety as quickly as possible was vital. Over time, our brains evolved to find pleasure in obtaining rewards without delay.

However, in today's world, where basic survival is less of a concern for many, this same psychological mechanism can lead to poor financial decisions. The brain doesn't always distinguish between a need and a want, so the feeling of reward or pleasure that comes from a purchase can feel just as satisfying as any survival-related gain our ancestors would have experienced.

In essence, our brains are hardwired to seek instant rewards. But while this served us well in primitive times, it is less helpful in a modern context where the long-term rewards of saving and investing are far more important than the instant gratification we get from impulsive spending.

Instant Gratification and Financial Decisions

The modern marketplace thrives on our desire for instant gratification. With online shopping, fast food, same-day delivery, and endless streaming services, we're constantly faced with opportunities to satisfy our immediate desires. Companies have perfected the art of making us feel that we need something *right now*, capitalizing on our psychology to increase sales and drive consumption.

The impact of instant gratification is evident in many of our day-to-day financial decisions:

- **Impulse Buying**: This is the most common example of instant gratification. How often have you bought something on a whim, only to regret it later? Impulse buying is driven by the need for immediate pleasure or the desire to avoid discomfort (e.g., the discomfort of waiting to make a purchase until it is truly necessary).

- **Subscription Services**: Services like Netflix, Spotify, Amazon Prime, and others tap into our craving for constant access to entertainment and convenience. The immediate pleasure of binge-watching a show or enjoying a playlist is incredibly satisfying, but the recurring monthly cost often goes unnoticed until it accumulates into a significant portion of our budget.

- **Fast Food and Convenience**: The rise of fast food chains and convenience stores plays into the instant gratification urge. The immediate satisfaction of eating something tasty or convenient often overshadows the long-term health consequences of poor eating habits, just as an impulsive purchase can overshadow the long-term financial impact of unnecessary spending.

- **Credit Cards and Buy Now, Pay Later Plans**: One of the most dangerous ways instant gratification impacts our spending is through credit. Credit cards and "Buy Now, Pay Later" plans allow consumers to buy things without paying upfront, which feels like immediate satisfaction. However, the financial strain of interest rates and delayed payments often leads to a cycle of debt, where the short-term pleasure of acquiring something is followed by long-term financial consequences.

Why We Can't Resist Instant Gratification

While the concept of instant gratification might seem simple, it's deeply ingrained in our habits and is reinforced by a variety of psychological mechanisms:

- **Dopamine and Reward System**: As mentioned earlier, dopamine is a key player in the pleasure-reward system. When we make a purchase, dopamine is released, making us feel good. Over time, our brain learns to associate buying things with pleasure, and it becomes a reinforcing cycle. Each time we buy something, we're rewarded with a dopamine hit, which reinforces the urge to buy more.

- **Cognitive Biases**: One of the cognitive biases that fuel instant gratification is the "present bias," which causes us to overvalue the present moment and undervalue the future. We tend to prioritize immediate rewards over long-term benefits, making it difficult to delay gratification even when we know that waiting will lead to a better outcome.

- **Social Influence and FOMO**: The pervasive culture of social media and advertising further exacerbates this tendency. Seeing others enjoy new products, vacations, or experiences can trigger a sense of urgency, leading to decisions driven by a fear of missing out (FOMO). This feeling is often exacerbated by social comparison, which compels us to keep up with the lifestyles we see on our feeds.

- **Escaping Discomfort**: Often, the desire for instant gratification is rooted in the need to alleviate discomfort. If we're feeling stressed, anxious, or bored, the temporary relief from shopping or indulging in a treat becomes a way to cope with negative emotions. This emotional spending, while providing immediate comfort, can lead to long-term financial stress and regret.

The Consequences of Instant Gratification

While chasing after instant pleasure might feel good in the moment, the long-term consequences can be damaging. Here are a few key areas where the impact of instant gratification can negatively affect our financial well-being:

1. **Accumulation of Debt**: The tendency to buy things on credit or indulge in purchases that

we can't afford leads to the accumulation of debt. What begins as a single impulse purchase can snowball into monthly credit card payments, high-interest rates, and financial stress.

2. **Missed Savings Goals**: The desire for instant gratification often gets in the way of long-term financial goals. Instead of saving money for retirement, buying a home, or building an emergency fund, we may spend the money on things that provide fleeting satisfaction, making it harder to achieve meaningful financial milestones.

3. **Emotional and Psychological Effects**: Instant gratification can also have emotional consequences. The initial happiness of making a purchase may quickly fade, leading to buyer's remorse or feelings of guilt. Over time, these feelings can accumulate, contributing to a sense of dissatisfaction or anxiety about finances.

4. **Lack of Financial Security**: A life lived in pursuit of instant rewards often leads to a lack of financial security. By focusing on short-term pleasures, we miss out on building a solid financial foundation that would provide lasting peace of mind.

Overcoming the Urge for Instant Gratification

Breaking free from the cycle of instant gratification requires developing the ability to delay rewards and shift our focus from short-term pleasure to long-term goals. Here are a few strategies to help overcome the urge for immediate rewards:

- **Practice Mindful Spending**: Before making a purchase, take a moment to pause and evaluate whether the item is truly necessary. Ask yourself if this purchase aligns with your financial goals, or if it's simply an emotional reaction to a temporary feeling.

- **Set Long-Term Goals**: Visualize your financial future and focus on the long-term rewards of saving and investing. When you feel the urge for immediate satisfaction, remind yourself of the bigger picture and the financial freedom you'll gain by delaying gratification.

- **Implement a 24-Hour Rule**: To curb impulse buying, set a rule for yourself: if you want to purchase something non-essential, wait 24 hours. This gives you time to reflect and determine if the item is truly worth the investment.

- **Replace Instant Gratification with Healthier Habits**: Find alternative ways to satisfy emotional or psychological needs that don't involve spending money. For example, instead of buying something to cope with stress, try exercising, meditating, or journaling.

- **Reward Yourself with Achievements**: Shift the focus from buying things to achieving personal goals. Reward yourself for sticking to a budget, saving a certain amount of money, or hitting a financial milestone, which will give you a sense of fulfillment without relying on material purchases.

Conclusion: Mastering the Urge for Instant Gratification

Instant gratification is a natural human tendency that, when left unchecked, can have long-lasting consequences on our financial health. However, with mindfulness, discipline, and a shift in perspective, we can learn to delay gratification and make decisions that align with our long-term financial goals. By recognizing the psychological forces behind instant gratification and implementing strategies to combat it, we can take control of our spending behavior and build a more secure and fulfilling financial future.

Chapter 4: The Power of Marketing and Advertising

Marketing and advertising are two of the most powerful forces in the modern world, influencing our thoughts, emotions, and purchasing decisions in ways we often don't even recognize. Every day, we're bombarded with hundreds of ads—on television, on social media, while browsing the internet, and even in the physical world. These ads are not just trying to sell us products—they're trying to sell us an idea, a lifestyle, a feeling. The impact of marketing is so pervasive that it shapes not just what we buy, but how we see ourselves, our values, and what we believe we *need* to be happy or successful.

In this chapter, we will explore how marketing and advertising shape our spending habits, from the psychological tricks they use to create urgency and desire to the deep emotional connections they forge with brands. We'll examine the powerful techniques that marketers and advertisers use to influence our choices and how we can become more aware of these tactics in order to make more informed, intentional decisions with our money.

The Psychology of Marketing: How Ads Target Our Minds

At its core, marketing is about influencing people's decisions by appealing to their emotions, desires, and sense of identity. Advertisers know that people don't make decisions based purely on logic. Instead, our purchasing choices are often driven by emotional triggers, social pressures, and psychological biases. To effectively influence consumer behavior, marketers use various psychological techniques that exploit these factors.

1. Creating Emotional Connections

One of the most powerful techniques in advertising is the creation of emotional connections between consumers and brands. This is why we often see ads that are not just about a product, but about how the product makes us feel. Think about the last commercial you saw that made you feel something—whether it was joy, nostalgia, or excitement. These ads use emotion to make the product feel like an essential part of your life.

For example, an ad for a luxury car may not just highlight the car's features; it might show a family driving through beautiful landscapes, laughing together, with soft music playing in the background. The message is clear: this car doesn't just take you from point A to point B—it brings you happiness, security, and connection. The emotional association with the car makes it seem more than just a mode of transportation; it becomes a symbol of success, family, and joy.

This emotional appeal is effective because it bypasses logical thinking and speaks directly to our desires and needs. By associating products with positive emotions, marketers are able to increase the perceived value of the product, which often leads to consumers justifying the purchase based on how it made them feel, rather than considering the practical aspects of the item.

2. Scarcity and Urgency: FOMO

Another psychological principle frequently used in marketing is the concept of scarcity. Scarcity taps into our fear of missing out (FOMO)–the anxiety that arises when we believe an opportunity is fleeting or limited. Whether it's a flash sale, a "limited edition" item, or the countdown timer on a website, marketers create a sense of urgency that encourages us to act quickly, often leading us to make impulse purchases.

The fear of missing out on something rare or exclusive triggers a sense of urgency that overrides careful consideration. Consider how many times you've bought something because it was "only available for the next 24 hours" or "while supplies last." The urgency makes the product feel more desirable, often convincing us to make a purchase we might not have otherwise considered.

This tactic is incredibly effective because it preys on our natural inclination to avoid loss. Behavioral economics tells us that losses tend to feel more painful than gains feel pleasurable, so the thought of losing out on an opportunity often leads to rash decisions. Marketers know this and use it to their advantage, making us feel that the item is not just desirable, but necessary.

3. Social Proof and Testimonials

Humans are social creatures, and we tend to look to others for guidance when making decisions. This phenomenon is known as social proof. In marketing, social proof is the idea that we are more likely to purchase a product if we see that others are using or recommending it.

One common example of social proof is the use of customer testimonials or reviews. When you see that a product has hundreds of glowing reviews or endorsements from "real people," it triggers the belief that this product is a "safe" choice, because other people have found it valuable. This is why influencers, celebrities, and social media endorsements have such an enormous impact on consumer behavior. If a well-known figure promotes a product, it instantly gains credibility, and consumers are more likely to trust that it's worth purchasing.

Marketers use social proof to make consumers feel like they are part of a larger community. Whether it's through user-generated content, influencer marketing, or customer testimonials, social proof creates the perception that if everyone else is doing it, it must be the right thing to do.

4. Anchoring and Pricing Techniques

Anchoring is a psychological bias that occurs when we rely too heavily on the first piece of information we encounter—often the initial price we see for a product or service. Marketers know that by setting a high initial price and then offering a discount, they can make the product appear to be a better deal, even if the original price was inflated to begin with.

For example, you might see a jacket with a "regular price" of $200, now "on sale" for $100. Even though you didn't intend to spend $200 on a jacket, the initial price serves as an anchor, making the $100 price tag feel like a steal, even if the item may not be worth that much.

This pricing strategy plays on the anchoring effect, making us feel like we're getting a great deal, even though the product may not have been worth the original price. The anchoring effect can be seen in a variety of settings, from retail stores to online shopping platforms, and it's one of the most effective ways to encourage consumers to buy.

The Role of Advertising in Shaping Our Identities

Advertising does more than just influence what we buy–it shapes who we think we are. Marketers understand that the products they sell are often tied to deeper desires and aspirations. For many consumers, purchasing certain products or brands is about creating or reinforcing their identity.

1. Branding and Self-Image

Brands have long been associated with identity. Think about the role that a brand like Apple plays in your sense of self. Apple's advertisements are carefully crafted to position their products as more than just technology–they represent innovation, simplicity, and status. People who buy Apple products aren't just purchasing a phone; they're buying into the idea of being cutting-edge and sophisticated. This is branding at its finest: positioning a product in such a way that it becomes an extension of the consumer's identity.

Similarly, other brands like Nike, Coca-Cola, and Louis Vuitton offer products that become synonymous with certain lifestyles or ideals. Nike doesn't just sell shoes; they sell the idea of athleticism, perseverance, and victory. Coca-Cola isn't just a beverage—it's a symbol of happiness, celebration, and togetherness. These brands have become woven into the fabric of our lives, not because of their inherent value but because of the identities they represent.

2. The Need for Belonging

Marketing often plays into our deep need for social connection and belonging. Advertisements frequently portray people enjoying their products in social settings, reinforcing the idea that purchasing these products will help us connect with others and be accepted by our peers. This desire for social acceptance is powerful—when we see advertisements that depict people using a product in a group or family setting, we naturally want to emulate that image.

The need for belonging has led to the rise of "tribal" branding, where people identify themselves with particular brands or products because they align with their values, lifestyle, or social group. For example, individuals who are passionate about sustainability may be drawn to eco-friendly brands, while those who value luxury and status might gravitate toward high-end products that communicate wealth.

How Marketing Manipulates Our Minds: Recognizing the Tactics

The techniques that marketers use are incredibly effective, but they're not foolproof. By becoming more aware of the tactics that advertisers employ, we can make more conscious decisions when it comes to spending money. Here are a few tips for recognizing and resisting the psychological tricks marketers use:

1. Question Your Emotional Responses

When you feel a strong emotional reaction to an ad—whether it's excitement, desire, or nostalgia—take a step back and ask yourself why you're feeling that way. Are you being influenced by an emotional appeal, or is the product truly something you need?

2. Practice Delayed Gratification

If you feel the urge to make an impulse purchase, give yourself a cooling-off period. Waiting 24 hours before making a purchase allows you to evaluate whether the item is truly worth the price or if it was just an emotional reaction to an ad.

3. Avoid Impulse Triggers

Turn off notifications for sales, unsubscribed from mailing lists, or unfollow accounts that trigger unnecessary purchases. The fewer advertisements you're exposed to, the less likely you'll be influenced by them.

4. Focus on Your Values

Instead of letting marketers shape your desires, focus on your own values and goals. Does the product align with your priorities? Is it something that will bring you closer to your long-term financial goals?

Conclusion: Taking Control of Your Spending in a Market-Driven World

Marketing and advertising are powerful forces that shape not just what we buy, but how we see ourselves and the world around us. By understanding the psychological tactics marketers use and becoming more aware of how they influence our spending decisions, we can take control of our financial choices. Instead of falling prey to the lure of immediate pleasure or societal pressures, we can make intentional, mindful decisions that align with our true needs and values.

Chapter 5: The Role of Fear and Scarcity

Fear is one of the most primal and powerful emotions we experience. It has the ability to compel us to act quickly, sometimes without thinking, in an effort to avoid perceived threats or to secure something we feel might be out of our reach. In the world of spending, fear manifests in subtle yet impactful ways, especially through the concepts of scarcity and the fear of missing out (FOMO). These feelings not only influence what we buy, but also how we value and prioritize our purchases.

This chapter explores the psychological mechanisms of fear and scarcity, detailing how they shape our spending behavior. From limited-time offers to the pressure of being left behind socially, we'll examine how fear plays a central role in consumer decision-making and how understanding these triggers can help us make smarter, more intentional choices with our money.

The Psychology of Scarcity: Why We Value What's Rare

Scarcity is a concept deeply embedded in human psychology. From an evolutionary standpoint, our ancestors valued resources that were rare because they were often critical for survival. If food, water, or shelter was in short supply, the ability to acquire and hoard those resources meant greater chances of survival. This instinct to place higher value on what is scarce has carried over into modern consumer behavior, where we continue to overvalue limited items, even if they don't serve an essential purpose.

1. The Scarcity Principle in Action

In today's marketplace, scarcity is often used as a marketing tactic to increase demand for products. Limited-edition releases, "while supplies last" offers, and exclusive items are all designed to tap into our innate sense of fear that we might lose out on something valuable. The simple fact that something is perceived as scarce can make it seem more valuable, even if the item itself is not inherently superior.

Think about the last time you saw a limited-time offer or a product labeled as "exclusive." You might have felt a slight rush to buy, even if the product wasn't something you particularly needed. This is because marketers have conditioned us to act quickly when we perceive something to be rare or in short supply. The feeling of urgency compels us to take action to avoid the discomfort of missing out.

For example, during Black Friday sales, retailers often advertise limited stock on certain items. The idea that only a certain number of items are available drives people to rush in and make purchases, even if they don't need the product. The scarcity effect influences our perception of the product's value, leading us to believe that we need to buy it now or risk losing the opportunity forever.

2. Fear of Missing Out (FOMO)

The fear of missing out (FOMO) is a psychological phenomenon where individuals feel anxiety about missing an opportunity, especially when they see others benefiting from it. FOMO is closely tied to scarcity in the marketplace, as marketers leverage this fear to drive consumer behavior. Whether it's the fear of missing out on a sale, a trendy product, or a limited-time offer, FOMO compels us to act quickly, often leading to purchases that are not well thought out.

FOMO is particularly strong in the context of social media, where we are constantly exposed to images of others enjoying experiences or products that seem desirable. Social media platforms create a constant cycle of comparison, where we see others enjoying new gadgets, going on exotic vacations, or wearing the latest fashion trends. This visibility can make us feel as though we're missing out if we don't keep up with the latest trends or acquisitions.

The fear of not being part of the "in crowd" can make us impulsively buy items, even if we don't really need them. For instance, seeing your friends post about a new tech gadget on Instagram might prompt you to buy one, not because it's essential, but because you fear being left out of the social conversation or experience. This is FOMO at work—making purchasing decisions based on emotional anxiety about missing an opportunity.

3. Social Proof and FOMO

FOMO is often amplified by social proof–the concept that we tend to follow the behavior of others, especially when we're uncertain about a decision. If we see our peers, family, or influencers endorsing a product or experience, we're more likely to desire it. This desire grows even stronger when we perceive that everyone else is benefiting from something we're not a part of. Social proof, coupled with scarcity, creates a perfect storm for impulsive buying.

Marketers exploit this combination of social proof and FOMO by showcasing customer testimonials, influencer endorsements, or social media trends. By making us feel like we're missing out on a valuable experience that everyone else is having, they can pressure us into making purchases quickly and without much reflection.

For example, an ad for a flash sale might feature images of happy customers, celebrities, or influencers using a product. This social proof makes us feel like we're part of an exclusive group, and the scarcity of the sale intensifies our fear of missing out. Together, these factors push us to act swiftly, sometimes resulting in buying things we hadn't originally planned on purchasing.

The Role of Urgency in Marketing

Urgency is another psychological tactic used to drive consumer behavior. When we perceive that an opportunity is fleeting, we tend to make decisions more quickly, often without the usual deliberation we'd employ if we thought we had more time. Marketers use urgency to create pressure, convincing us that if we don't act now, we may never get the chance again.

1. Limited-Time Offers and Flash Sales

Limited-time offers and flash sales are one of the most common strategies used to create urgency. By setting a time limit on a sale, marketers encourage us to make quicker decisions. We feel the pressure to act fast, even if we don't need the product. These sales often come with high discounts or additional bonuses that make us believe we're getting an exceptional deal.

For example, the phrase "24-Hour Flash Sale" or "Only 5 Left at This Price" is designed to create a sense of urgency that pushes us to act before the opportunity disappears. The fear of missing out on the deal can override our rational thinking, leading us to buy things we may not have considered if given more time to think about the purchase.

2. Countdown Timers and "Last Chance" Warnings

Many websites now feature countdown timers for sales, promotions, and special offers. These timers create a sense of urgency by showing us how much time is left before an offer expires. The countdown intensifies the fear of missing out and compels us to act quickly.

Similarly, phrases like "Last Chance" or "Final Offer" are designed to make us feel like this is our only opportunity to get the product at a certain price. These tactics trigger a fear-based response, which makes us act impulsively and make decisions based on urgency rather than necessity.

Scarcity and Emotional Spending

The relationship between scarcity, fear, and emotional spending is an important one. Often, the fear of losing out or missing out triggers emotional buying behavior—where people purchase items not because they truly need them, but because they feel an emotional need to act quickly. This behavior can be particularly dangerous in the context of long-term financial health.

1. Instant Gratification and Long-Term Consequences

Scarcity-based marketing plays into the concept of instant gratification, which we explored in an earlier chapter. When an item is framed as rare or limited, the desire to own it immediately can be overwhelming. This impulse to buy in the moment, driven by the fear of missing out, can lead to long-term financial consequences such as accumulating debt or straining personal finances.

For example, you might purchase an expensive handbag during a flash sale, thinking it's a great deal, only to realize later that it wasn't a necessary purchase, and it puts a strain on your budget. The immediate satisfaction of owning the item is often short-lived, but the financial repercussions can last much longer.

2. Overcoming the Fear of Missing Out

To counteract the influence of fear and scarcity in marketing, it's important to develop strategies for resisting impulse buys driven by FOMO. Here are a few methods for doing so:

- **Pause and Reflect**: When you feel the urge to make a quick purchase, pause and take a moment to reflect. Ask yourself whether the item is truly necessary or if it's just the fear of missing out influencing your decision. Waiting for 24 to 48 hours can help you evaluate whether the purchase aligns with your long-term goals or if it's just an emotional reaction.

- **Remind Yourself of Your Goals**: Establishing long-term financial goals can help you stay focused on what truly matters. When faced with a scarcity-driven purchase, remind yourself of your larger objectives, such as saving for a home, paying off debt, or building an emergency fund.

- **Limit Exposure**: One of the best ways to avoid succumbing to the pressure of scarcity is to limit your exposure to marketing tactics. Unsubscribe from mailing lists, disable notifications for sales, and avoid browsing sites that tempt you with limited-time offers.

- **Focus on Value**: Instead of being swayed by the urgency of a sale, focus on the actual value of the product. Ask yourself if it's something you'll use regularly or if it's simply an impulse buy that you'll regret later.

Conclusion: Navigating the Fear and Scarcity Trap

Fear and scarcity are powerful forces that marketers use to manipulate consumer behavior. By understanding how these psychological triggers influence our spending habits, we can become more aware of the tactics that push us into making impulsive decisions. While scarcity and urgency can create a sense of excitement and desire, it's important to remember that not every limited-time offer is a true opportunity. By practicing mindfulness, setting clear financial goals, and resisting the urge to buy out of fear, we can take control of our spending and make more intentional, fulfilling financial choices.

Chapter 6: Consumerism and Its Impact on Identity

In the modern world, the act of consumption is not just about acquiring products—it's deeply entwined with how we define ourselves, our values, and our social identity. Consumerism, the cultural phenomenon of continually acquiring goods and services, has evolved into much more than a means of survival or convenience. It's now a way to signal who we are, what we stand for, and where we fit within society. The products we buy, the brands we support, and the way we present ourselves through material possessions have come to shape not just our lives, but our sense of self.

In this chapter, we'll explore how consumerism affects our personal identity, from the way we use products as symbols of social status and belonging to the deeper psychological motivations that drive our desire for material goods. We'll examine the concept of identity in a consumer-driven society, how brands influence our self-image, and how we can take back control of our identity by understanding and redefining our relationship with consumption.

Consumerism: More Than Just Buying Things

At its core, consumerism is about more than simply buying goods–it's about the symbolic meaning attached to those goods. Consumerism has become a central force in shaping modern identity because what we buy often signals our values, lifestyle choices, and status. From the clothes we wear to the car we drive, each purchase we make has the potential to communicate something about who we are and what we aspire to be.

In the past, consumption was largely a matter of necessity. People bought what they needed to survive and function in society. In today's consumer-driven society, however, consumption has become more about desire than necessity. People buy not just to meet practical needs but to project an image of themselves to others. This shift has created a culture where identity is often defined by what we consume rather than who we are.

1. Consumption as a Status Symbol

One of the most significant ways consumerism impacts our identity is through its role as a status symbol. The desire to convey a certain image or social status often drives purchasing decisions. In many cases, the products we buy are not just about personal enjoyment; they're about signaling to others that we belong to a certain group, class, or lifestyle.

For example, owning a luxury car, wearing high-end fashion brands, or living in an upscale neighborhood can serve as a way to express wealth, success, and social prestige. These products, while functional, are imbued with symbolic value. They become markers of one's social standing, a way to communicate to others that you've "made it." The pursuit of status through consumption is not confined to the wealthy–it's pervasive across all socioeconomic classes, as people from different walks of life seek to "keep up" with the latest trends and material symbols of success.

This desire for status is often reinforced by advertising, which associates certain products with success and fulfillment. A commercial for a luxury watch, for example, might not only show the watch but also associate it with a life of elegance, adventure, and prestige. The message is clear: purchasing this product will not just improve your life; it will elevate your status and align you with a certain identity.

2. The Pressure of Social Comparison

Another powerful force in consumerism is social comparison. Humans have an inherent tendency to compare themselves to others, especially in terms of material possessions. Social comparison theory, proposed by psychologist Leon Festinger, suggests that we evaluate our own worth by comparing ourselves to others. This comparison often influences our purchasing decisions as we try to match or surpass the lifestyles of those around us.

Social media, with its curated posts and influencer-driven culture, has amplified the pressure to keep up with others. Platforms like Instagram, Facebook, and TikTok are filled with images of idealized lives–vacations, luxury items, designer clothes, and experiences that seem out of reach for many people.

These platforms create a sense of social comparison, leading individuals to feel that they need to purchase similar items or experiences to fit in or to be seen as successful.

The pressure to keep up with others can lead to overspending, as people try to match the material possessions of their peers. It's not uncommon to make purchases based on social pressure rather than personal need or desire. This can lead to financial strain and, over time, feelings of inadequacy or dissatisfaction, as the pursuit of material goods becomes an endless cycle of comparison and consumption.

Branding and Its Role in Shaping Identity

Brands have an extraordinary ability to shape our sense of self. Through marketing, branding, and storytelling, companies don't just sell products—they sell identities. Successful brands are able to create an emotional connection with consumers, positioning themselves as more than just a product or service. They represent a lifestyle, an aspiration, or a way of being.

1. Brands as Personal Identity Markers

From Apple to Nike, Coca-Cola to Tesla, brands have become symbols of identity and self-expression. People don't just buy a product; they buy into the idea of what that product represents. Apple, for example, isn't just selling a phone–it's selling an identity of innovation, simplicity, and modernity. Nike doesn't just sell sportswear; it sells the identity of an athlete, someone who pushes boundaries and strives for greatness.

This deep connection between brands and identity is particularly prevalent in consumer culture. The brands we choose to support reflect our values, desires, and self-perception. When we purchase a product, we're not just choosing a commodity; we're signaling something about who we are. For some, this identity might be tied to status–choosing high-end brands that symbolize wealth or exclusivity. For others, it might be about aligning with a certain philosophy or lifestyle, such as eco-conscious or socially responsible brands.

For example, when you purchase a product from Patagonia, you're not just buying clothing–you're aligning yourself with the brand's values of environmental sustainability and ethical practices. Similarly, owning a Tesla doesn't just signify owning an electric car; it symbolizes a commitment to innovation, environmental awareness, and a futuristic vision of society. Brands like these appeals to our deeper desires to express who we are through our consumption choices.

2. The Power of Emotional Branding

Emotional branding takes this connection to a deeper level. Instead of simply showcasing the features of a product, emotional branding connects with consumers on a personal and emotional level. Successful brands evoke feelings—whether it's excitement, nostalgia, or a sense of belonging.

Coca-Cola, for example, has long associated its brand with happiness, togetherness, and joy. Their commercials, especially during the holiday season, are filled with scenes of family gatherings, celebrations, and moments of connection. The brand doesn't just sell a sugary drink; it sells the feeling of shared happiness and celebration. By connecting with consumers emotionally, Coca-Cola has created a brand that represents more than just a product—it represents an idealized version of life.

This emotional connection is a potent force. When we buy products that resonate with us on an emotional level, we are reinforcing certain aspects of our identity. For example, people who identify with a sense of adventure and freedom may be drawn to brands like Jeep or The North Face, which evoke these qualities through their marketing and imagery. In this way, consumerism shapes not just what we own, but the person we believe ourselves to be.

Consumerism and the Search for Meaning

In a consumer-driven society, there is a growing emphasis on "having" over "being." Many people turn to material possessions in an effort to define themselves, fill emotional voids, or seek validation from others. This often leads to what psychologists call "materialism"—the belief that happiness, success, and fulfillment can be achieved through the accumulation of material goods.

1. The Pursuit of Happiness through Consumption

A central tenet of consumerism is the idea that buying things will bring happiness. Advertisements often promise that owning a product will make us feel better, look better, or live a better life. This pursuit of happiness through consumption is pervasive in modern society, but research shows that material wealth does not necessarily correlate with increased happiness or well-being. In fact, studies have shown that people who are highly materialistic tend to have lower levels of life satisfaction and greater emotional distress.

This disconnection between material goods and lasting happiness can create a cycle of consumption in which people buy more and more, yet still feel unfulfilled. The pursuit of happiness through acquisition is often fleeting, and the satisfaction gained from a new product quickly fades, leading to the need for more possessions to fill the gap.

2. The Trap of Consumerism and Identity Crisis

One of the dangers of consumerism is that it encourages people to define themselves based on what they have rather than who they are. People who derive their self-worth from their possessions may find that their identity is fragile and dependent on external validation. If they can't afford the latest trends, they might feel left out or inferior. If they can't live up to the image they've created through their purchases, they might experience feelings of inadequacy or self-doubt.

This reliance on material goods for identity can lead to an identity crisis. When someone loses their job, goes through a financial setback, or is unable to keep up with the latest trends, their sense of self can be shaken. The external validation they once received from their possessions no longer provides the same sense of security, leaving them to grapple with questions about who they truly are without the comfort of consumerism.

Taking Back Control: Redefining Your Identity Beyond Consumerism

The first step in reclaiming control over our identity in a consumer-driven society is to become aware of the ways in which consumerism influences our sense of self. We need to ask ourselves: *Do the products we own truly define who we are, or are they simply reflections of external pressures and cultural conditioning?*

1. Reflecting on Values, Not Brands

To break free from the cycle of consumerism, it's important to reconnect with our core values rather than letting brands define us. What truly matters to you—relationships, personal growth, experiences, or creativity? When we focus on what truly brings fulfillment, we can shift our attention away from consumer-driven ideals and begin to build a more meaningful and authentic identity.

2. Practicing Minimalism and Intentional Living

One way to combat the identity-based pressures of consumerism is to embrace minimalism. This doesn't mean rejecting all material possessions, but rather, being intentional about what we own and why. By choosing to keep only the things that bring us true value and joy, we can free ourselves from the clutter of unnecessary consumption and focus on what really contributes to our well-being.

Conclusion: Finding Identity Beyond Material Goods

Consumerism has a powerful influence on our sense of identity, shaping not only what we own but how we see ourselves and how we wish to be seen by others. By becoming more mindful of the forces that drive our purchasing decisions, we can begin to redefine our identities beyond material possessions and external validation. When we move away from the belief that happiness and fulfillment come from what we own, we can discover a deeper sense of self that is not dependent on consumption. In the following chapters, we'll continue to explore how we can take control of our financial lives by understanding the psychological forces that influence our spending habits, and how we can build a healthier, more intentional relationship with money.

Chapter 7: Habitual Spending

Spending habits are like invisible forces that drive much of our daily financial behavior. They can be as automatic as brushing our teeth in the morning or as ingrained as reaching for our phones the moment we feel bored. While some spending is driven by conscious decisions and needs, habitual spending often operates below the surface, driven by routines, comfort, and subconscious triggers. Over time, these habits accumulate and become harder to break, leaving us trapped in a cycle of mindless purchases.

In this chapter, we will explore the psychology behind habitual spending, the factors that contribute to developing these habits, and how they can negatively impact our financial well-being. More importantly, we will discuss strategies for breaking free from these patterns, empowering you to develop healthier spending behaviors and regain control of your financial future.

What is Habitual Spending?

Habitual spending refers to the tendency to make purchases on a regular basis without giving much thought to whether the items are truly needed or aligned with your financial goals. These purchases often become so routine that they feel automatic, like an unthinking part of your day. For example, buying a cup of coffee every morning before work, ordering takeout for dinner every Friday night, or subscribing to a streaming service that you rarely use—these types of habitual spending behaviors can accumulate over time, draining your finances and preventing you from reaching your long-term goals.

At its core, habitual spending is often driven by convenience, comfort, or emotional reward. We become so accustomed to certain spending behaviors that they feel like a natural part of our daily lives, whether or not they actually contribute to our overall well-being or financial security. The challenge is that these habits are not always aligned with our true needs or desires. They are simply routines that have developed over time, often without much thought.

How Habitual Spending Develops

Habitual spending doesn't happen overnight. It's the result of repeated behavior over time, reinforced by external cues, emotional triggers, and psychological rewards. Let's take a closer look at how these habits are formed:

1. Routine and Convenience

One of the most common reasons for habitual spending is routine. Human beings are creatures of habit, and once a certain behavior becomes part of our daily or weekly routine, it's easy to fall into a cycle of mindless spending. For example, grabbing a coffee every morning on your way to work might start as a treat, but over time, it becomes an ingrained part of your day. The convenience of stopping at your local coffee shop every morning makes it effortless to continue the behavior, even if you don't consciously evaluate whether it's a necessary purchase.

Routines are comforting because they create predictability in our lives. However, when those routines involve spending money, it can lead to unnecessary or excessive purchases that add up over time. The ease of continuing these routines, without actively considering alternatives, reinforces the habit and makes it harder to break free.

2. Emotional Triggers

Emotions play a powerful role in the development of spending habits. Many people develop spending habits as a way to cope with stress, anxiety, boredom, or even feelings of happiness. For example, someone might buy new clothes when they're feeling down as a way to lift their spirits, or they might treat themselves to a nice dinner after a long workweek as a reward. In these cases, the purchase is often more about the emotional satisfaction or reward than the actual need for the item.

Over time, these emotional triggers become linked to certain spending behaviors. The more we associate spending with positive emotional outcomes (even if fleeting), the more likely we are to repeat that behavior in the future. This emotional connection can make habitual spending even harder to break, as it's tied to deeper psychological needs and feelings.

3. Social and Cultural Pressures

Social influence is another powerful force behind habitual spending. The people we interact with, our social circles, and the larger cultural environment in which we live all influence our spending behaviors. For example, if everyone around you regularly goes out to lunch or spends money on the latest gadgets, you might feel pressured to do the same to fit in or keep up. The constant exposure to these behaviors, whether through friends, family, or social media, creates a sense of normalization around certain spending habits.

Cultural expectations also play a role. In many cultures, certain purchases are seen as necessary or expected, regardless of whether they align with an individual's financial goals. For example, the pressure to celebrate holidays or birthdays with lavish gifts, or to host extravagant parties, can drive habitual spending. Over time, these social and cultural pressures can shape the way we view spending, reinforcing the idea that it's normal or even necessary to spend money in certain ways.

The Impact of Habitual Spending

Habitual spending may seem harmless at first, but over time, it can have significant financial consequences. Let's look at some of the ways habitual spending can negatively affect your financial health:

1. Erosion of Savings and Financial Goals

One of the most immediate consequences of habitual spending is the erosion of your savings and the slow progress toward your financial goals. Small, recurring expenses—whether it's a daily coffee, an unused subscription service, or weekly takeout—might seem trivial on their own. However, when these small purchases add up over time, they can drain your disposable income and prevent you from saving for more important goals like retirement, buying a home, or building an emergency fund.

If you're not mindful of these recurring expenses, they can sneakily eat away at your budget, leaving you with little to put toward long-term financial security. The result is a lack of progress toward the things that truly matter, like financial freedom or a stable future.

2. Increased Debt and Financial Stress

Habitual spending, especially when it's not aligned with your income, can lead to debt accumulation. If you rely on credit cards or loans to finance regular purchases, you're adding to your debt every month. Over time, this can lead to a cycle of borrowing and repaying, which can become overwhelming and stressful. As interest accrues on your debts, you may find yourself paying much more than the original cost of the items you've bought, making it even harder to regain control of your finances.

The stress of managing debt, combined with the guilt of spending money on unnecessary items, can create a vicious cycle of financial anxiety. This anxiety, in turn, can fuel more emotional spending, further exacerbating the problem.

3. Limited Financial Flexibility

Habitual spending often leads to a lack of financial flexibility. When a large portion of your income is dedicated to routine or non-essential purchases, you have less room to respond to unexpected financial challenges. Emergencies, such as medical bills, car repairs, or sudden job loss, can be much harder to handle if you're locked into spending patterns that drain your resources.

In contrast, individuals who make a conscious effort to reduce habitual spending often have greater financial flexibility. By consciously redirecting funds from non-essential purchases to savings, investing, or paying down debt, they create a cushion that can protect them from life's financial uncertainties.

Breaking Free from Habitual Spending

Breaking free from habitual spending requires mindfulness, self-awareness, and a commitment to creating new, healthier spending habits. Here are some strategies that can help you regain control:

1. Track Your Spending

The first step in breaking any spending habit is to become aware of it. Keeping a record of your expenses for a month or two can help you see where your money is going. By tracking your purchases, you can identify patterns of habitual spending—whether it's a daily coffee run, a monthly subscription, or spontaneous online shopping.

Once you've identified these habits, you can start to evaluate whether they align with your financial goals. Are these purchases bringing you long-term happiness or value, or are they simply a way to fill emotional gaps or pass time?

2. Set Specific Financial Goals

Having clear, specific financial goals can help you reframe your spending habits. When you know exactly what you're working toward—whether it's paying off debt, building an emergency fund, or saving for a vacation—you're more likely to make intentional spending decisions that align with your goals. Set both short-term and long-term goals, and use them as a motivator to resist impulsive purchases.

3. Replace Bad Habits with Positive Alternatives

To break free from habitual spending, it's helpful to replace unhealthy habits with more productive ones. For example, if you habitually buy coffee every morning, consider making your coffee at home or trying a new morning ritual, like going for a walk or meditating. If you often order takeout, try cooking at home with simple, inexpensive recipes.

By replacing old habits with new, intentional ones, you can reduce your dependence on spending as a form of comfort or routine. Over time, these new habits will become just as automatic as your old ones, but with a positive financial impact.

4. Limit Exposure to Temptation

If you find it difficult to resist habitual spending, limit your exposure to the triggers that prompt it. Unsubscribe from marketing emails, avoid browsing online stores, and minimize social media exposure to ads or influencers that tempt you to spend. By reducing the opportunities for impulsive purchases, you can break free from the cycle of habitual spending.

Conclusion: Regaining Control of Your Financial Future

Habitual spending is a powerful force that can sneak into your life without you even realizing it. It's often driven by routine, emotional needs, and external pressures, making it difficult to break free from. However, by becoming aware of these habits, tracking your spending, setting clear financial goals, and replacing old patterns with new, healthier behaviors, you can take control of your financial future.

Chapter 8: Emotional Spending and Coping Mechanisms

Emotional spending is one of the most insidious forms of consumer behavior. Unlike spending driven by practical needs or rational decision-making, emotional spending is often fueled by feelings—whether it's stress, anxiety, sadness, or even happiness. When we purchase items to cope with emotions rather than real needs, we're not just engaging in a financial transaction; we're attempting to find emotional relief. However, while emotional spending may offer temporary comfort, it often leads to long-term financial distress and regret.

In this chapter, we will explore the psychology of emotional spending, the reasons why we use consumption as a coping mechanism, and how this behavior can spiral into financial problems. More importantly, we will discuss strategies for breaking the cycle of emotional spending and developing healthier coping mechanisms that don't rely on retail therapy.

What is Emotional Spending?

Emotional spending occurs when a person buys something to satisfy an emotional need rather than a practical one. This form of spending is often a response to emotional triggers such as stress, boredom, anxiety, loneliness, or even happiness. Unlike rational purchases—like buying groceries, paying bills, or purchasing necessary items—emotional purchases are driven by the desire for instant gratification, temporary relief, or a quick mood boost.

For example, you might purchase a new pair of shoes to cheer yourself up after a rough day at work, or splurge on a meal at your favorite restaurant when you're feeling lonely. While the purchase may bring temporary pleasure or distraction, it doesn't address the underlying emotional issue. In fact, emotional spending can lead to feelings of guilt or regret later, exacerbating the very emotions you were trying to avoid in the first place.

Why Do We Turn to Emotional Spending?

Understanding the reasons behind emotional spending is key to addressing the root causes of this behavior. Several psychological and emotional factors contribute to the tendency to use spending as a coping mechanism:

1. Instant Gratification

One of the most powerful drivers of emotional spending is the desire for instant gratification. In times of emotional distress, it can be tempting to make a purchase that offers immediate relief. Whether it's a shopping spree, a new gadget, or an indulgent treat, spending money can provide a brief, pleasurable distraction from negative emotions. The act of buying something new triggers the release of dopamine in the brain, which gives us a temporary "high"—a quick fix that can feel satisfying in the moment.

However, this rush of pleasure is fleeting. Once the item is purchased and the initial excitement fades, the emotional discomfort that triggered the purchase often returns. This cycle of emotional spending and temporary relief becomes self-reinforcing, making it harder to break free.

2. Avoidance of Negative Emotions

Many people turn to emotional spending as a way to avoid dealing with difficult emotions. When feelings like sadness, stress, or frustration arise, spending money becomes a way to escape or numb those emotions. It's easier to buy something new than to confront the underlying cause of the negative feeling. This is particularly true for people who struggle with emotional regulation or who are uncomfortable with emotional discomfort.

For instance, someone experiencing anxiety might buy a new item as a way to temporarily distract themselves from their worries. Similarly, a person going through a breakup might buy a luxury item to fill the emotional void left by the end of the relationship. While the purchase may provide short-term relief, it doesn't solve the root issue and often leads to greater emotional turmoil and financial strain.

3. Rewarding Ourselves

Emotional spending can also occur as a form of self-reward. People often turn to shopping or indulgence when they feel they've earned a reward, especially after completing a challenging task or experiencing personal success. For instance, after finishing a major work project or achieving a personal goal, someone might feel justified in treating themselves to a shopping spree or a night out.

While rewarding ourselves is a natural and healthy practice, it becomes problematic when the rewards are disproportionate to the achievement or are used as a way to justify excessive spending. When we repeatedly use purchases as a form of reward, it can quickly spiral into habitual emotional spending.

4. Social Comparison and FOMO

In today's world of constant social media exposure, the pressure to keep up with others can drive emotional spending. Seeing friends, influencers, or celebrities showcasing their latest purchases or experiences can trigger feelings of inadequacy or the fear of missing out (FOMO). This social comparison leads people to buy things not because they genuinely want or need them, but because they feel they need to measure up to others.

The desire to fit in, maintain an image, or project a certain lifestyle can cause people to overspend in order to keep up with their social circles. Whether it's purchasing the latest fashion trends, going on an

expensive vacation, or dining at trendy restaurants, FOMO can be a powerful emotional trigger that leads to unnecessary spending.

The Consequences of Emotional Spending

While emotional spending may provide temporary relief, it often leads to long-term financial and emotional consequences. Here are some of the most significant drawbacks of using spending as a coping mechanism:

1. Accumulating Debt

One of the most immediate consequences of emotional spending is the accumulation of debt. If spending is consistently driven by emotions rather than need, it can result in overspending, which often requires using credit cards or loans to cover the costs. Over time, the debt can build up, leading to interest charges, late fees, and a cycle of borrowing to cover previous purchases. This debt can quickly spiral out of control, creating additional stress and anxiety.

2. Buyer's Remorse and Guilt

After making an emotional purchase, many people experience buyer's remorse–the feeling of regret that arises once the initial excitement fades. This guilt can be compounded by the realization that the purchase was made impulsively, without careful thought or consideration. The emotional high of the

purchase dissipates, and the underlying emotions (stress, loneliness, or boredom) remain, making the person feel even worse about their decision.

This cycle of emotional spending followed by regret can create a negative feedback loop, where people continue to buy in an attempt to fill the emotional void, only to experience guilt and dissatisfaction afterward.

3. Undermining Long-Term Financial Goals

Emotional spending can also derail long-term financial goals. When spending is driven by emotions, it often leads to unplanned or excessive purchases, which can make it harder to save for important financial milestones. Saving for retirement, buying a house, or building an emergency fund can feel less urgent when we're focused on the immediate gratification of a new purchase.

Over time, this can lead to financial instability, as people prioritize short-term desires over long-term security. The more you engage in emotional spending, the more difficult it becomes to stick to a budget or maintain financial discipline.

4. Emotional Rollercoaster

Ironically, emotional spending can exacerbate the very emotions you're trying to avoid. While the initial purchase may offer relief, it doesn't address the root cause of the emotional distress. In fact, the financial consequences of overspending often create

additional stress, anxiety, or feelings of inadequacy. Instead of solving the problem, emotional spending can compound it, leading to a cycle of emotional highs and lows that are difficult to break.

Breaking the Cycle of Emotional Spending

The key to overcoming emotional spending is to address the underlying emotional triggers and replace unhealthy coping mechanisms with healthier alternatives. Here are some strategies that can help you break the cycle of emotional spending:

1. Identify Emotional Triggers

The first step in overcoming emotional spending is to identify the emotional triggers that lead to impulsive purchases. Are you more likely to spend when you're feeling stressed, bored, lonely, or anxious? Keeping a journal or tracking your spending can help you pinpoint when and why you tend to spend emotionally.

Once you identify these triggers, you can work on finding healthier ways to cope with your emotions. For example, if stress leads you to shop for comfort, try deep breathing exercises, yoga, or taking a walk as an alternative. The goal is to find ways to manage your emotions without relying on retail therapy.

2. Develop Mindful Spending Habits

Mindful spending involves being fully aware of your financial decisions and ensuring that purchases align with your values and goals. Before making a purchase, ask yourself whether the item is truly necessary or if it's being bought as a way to cope with an emotional state. Waiting 24 hours before making a non-essential purchase can give you time to reflect and determine if the item is worth buying.

By practicing mindful spending, you become more intentional with your purchases, making sure they are motivated by need rather than emotion.

3. Build Healthy Coping Mechanisms

Instead of turning to spending as a way to manage emotions, focus on building healthier coping mechanisms. Exercise, journaling, meditation, and connecting with friends or family are all effective ways to process emotions without spending money. Finding activities that bring you joy and fulfillment—without the need to shop—can help you break the emotional spending cycle.

4. Set Financial Boundaries

Establishing financial boundaries is crucial for preventing emotional spending. Set a monthly budget and allocate specific amounts for discretionary spending. If you feel the urge to make an emotional purchase, check your budget first to see if it fits within your financial limits. Setting limits on how much you can spend on non-essential items can help you stay on track with your long-term financial goals.

Conclusion: Creating a Healthier Relationship with Money

Emotional spending is a natural response to difficult emotions, but when it becomes a regular habit, it can have serious financial consequences. By understanding the emotional triggers that lead to impulsive purchases, developing healthier coping mechanisms, and practicing mindful spending, you can break free from the cycle of emotional buying and build a more positive, sustainable relationship with money.

Chapter 9: The Psychology of Money in Relationships

Money is often referred to as one of the leading causes of stress in relationships, and for good reason. Our financial habits, beliefs, and attitudes can deeply affect the dynamics between partners, family members, and friends. Whether it's disagreements over spending, differing views on saving, or financial secrets, money can become a point of tension that undermines trust and harmony. Yet, as much as money can create conflict, it can also serve as a source of bonding and shared goals when managed well.

In this chapter, we will explore the psychology of money in relationships, examining how individuals' financial behaviors and attitudes are shaped by their upbringing, cultural background, and personality traits. We will also discuss how money-related conflicts arise in relationships, the impact of financial stress, and how couples and families can foster open, healthy discussions about money. The goal is not only to understand how money affects relationships but also to provide practical strategies for building stronger, more supportive financial partnerships.

The Role of Money in Relationships

Money is more than just a tool for purchasing goods and services–it is deeply intertwined with our sense of security, status, and identity. How we handle money often reflects our values, priorities, and fears.

In relationships, these financial attitudes and behaviors can clash, creating friction and misunderstandings.

For example, one partner may view money as a means to achieve security and stability, while the other may see it as a tool for freedom and enjoyment. These differing perspectives on money can lead to conflicts about budgeting, spending, saving, and long-term financial planning. Even in the most loving relationships, money can quickly become a source of tension if both partners are not aligned in their financial goals and priorities.

How Money Attitudes Are Shaped

Our attitudes toward money are shaped by a variety of factors, many of which are established in childhood. Early life experiences, cultural conditioning, and family dynamics play a key role in how we view money and how we manage it as adults. Understanding these influences can help us recognize why we, and our partners, behave the way we do when it comes to finances.

1. Family Upbringing

One of the most significant influences on our financial attitudes is how we were raised. The way our parents or caregivers handled money, whether consciously or unconsciously, teaches us valuable (or harmful) lessons about money management. For example, children who grew up in families that struggled financially may develop a scarcity mindset—constantly fearing that there won't be enough money to go around. On the other hand, children who grew up in affluent households may develop a sense of entitlement or a tendency to overspend, thinking that money is always available.

In relationships, these early lessons can create mismatches in financial expectations. A partner who grew up in a frugal household may feel uncomfortable with their spouse's tendency to spend freely, while someone raised in a more indulgent environment might struggle to understand why their partner is so cautious with money.

2. Cultural and Societal Influences

Cultural norms and societal values also play a critical role in shaping our approach to money. Different cultures have different attitudes toward wealth, debt, and financial independence. For example, in some cultures, collective family support is prioritized, and wealth is shared among extended family members. In others, individual financial independence is a core value, and people are expected to manage their own finances without relying on family assistance.

These cultural differences can create challenges in relationships where partners come from different backgrounds. What one person sees as a reasonable financial expectation might seem unusual or even unfair to someone with a different cultural perspective.

3. Personal Experiences and Personality

Our personal experiences and personality traits also influence our financial behavior. For instance, someone who has experienced financial hardship might be more conservative with money, whereas someone who has experienced financial freedom or success might be more inclined to take risks with spending or investing. Personality traits, such as impulsiveness, risk tolerance, and the need for control, also play a role in how we approach money.

A partner who is more spontaneous and prone to impulse buys may clash with a partner who is meticulous about budgeting and saving. These differing tendencies can lead to conflict if not addressed or understood.

Money Conflicts in Relationships

Money conflicts are a common issue in relationships, and these disputes can range from minor disagreements to serious, relationship-threatening problems. Understanding the root causes of money conflicts is essential for resolving them effectively.

1. Differing Financial Priorities

One of the most common sources of conflict in relationships is differing financial priorities. In an ideal world, both partners would have a shared vision for their financial future. However, in reality, individuals often have different financial goals based on their upbringing, personality, and life experiences.

For example, one partner might prioritize saving for retirement or paying off debt, while the other might prefer spending money on vacations, hobbies, or other experiences. These differences can create tension, as one partner may feel that their goals are being sidelined or disregarded by the other.

2. Power Struggles and Control

Money can also become a tool for power and control in relationships. When one partner earns significantly more than the other, it can create an imbalance of power that affects how financial decisions are made. In some cases, the higher-earning partner may use their income as leverage to control spending, decision-making, or even the other partner's sense of independence.

Similarly, some individuals may feel a need to control every aspect of their partner's financial life, which can lead to resentment and emotional distance. On the flip side, one partner may refuse to discuss money matters altogether, leaving the other partner in the dark about their financial situation.

3. Financial Stress and Anxiety

Financial stress is another major contributor to conflict in relationships. Money worries, such as debt, job loss, or inadequate savings, can lead to anxiety, frustration, and feelings of helplessness. This stress often spills over into the relationship, causing arguments, emotional distance, and resentment. Financial difficulties can also strain communication, making it harder for couples to discuss their concerns and work together toward solutions.

Financial stress can also exacerbate other emotional issues in the relationship. For example, a partner who is feeling anxious about money may become more irritable, withdrawn, or defensive, which can affect the overall dynamics of the relationship.

How to Foster Healthy Financial Conversations

Addressing money issues in relationships requires open, honest, and respectful communication. By creating a space for discussing financial matters, couples can build trust, avoid misunderstandings, and work toward common financial goals. Here are some strategies for fostering healthier financial conversations:

1. Establish Shared Financial Goals

One of the first steps in resolving money conflicts is to sit down and discuss your shared financial goals. Whether it's saving for a house, planning for retirement, or creating an emergency fund, having a clear, shared vision can help align your financial priorities. Once you agree on your goals, you can work together to create a budget or financial plan that supports these objectives.

Regularly revisiting and adjusting these goals is also important, as financial circumstances and priorities can change over time. By having a joint vision, you can both feel like you are working toward the same outcomes.

2. Set Clear Boundaries and Roles

In relationships, it's important to set clear boundaries and responsibilities when it comes to finances. Who will manage the budget? Who will track expenses? Will you combine finances, or will each partner maintain separate accounts? Having these conversations upfront can help avoid misunderstandings and reduce conflict.

In some relationships, it might be helpful to assign specific roles based on each partner's strengths and preferences. For example, if one partner is more financially savvy, they may take on the responsibility of managing investments or retirement planning, while the other partner might handle day-to-day expenses or household budgeting.

3. Practice Transparency and Honesty

Transparency and honesty are key when it comes to money in relationships. Hiding financial problems, debts, or purchases from a partner can create mistrust and resentment. It's important to regularly communicate about finances, discuss any financial concerns, and address issues before they escalate.

Being open about financial mistakes or challenges can help create a sense of partnership, where both individuals are working together to resolve issues. It's essential to have a no-judgment, supportive attitude during these discussions so that both partners feel comfortable sharing their thoughts and concerns.

4. Learn to Compromise

In any relationship, compromise is essential, and the same holds true when it comes to money. If you and your partner have different financial priorities or habits, finding middle ground is key. Perhaps one partner loves to travel, while the other prefers saving for the future. Compromise might involve budgeting for both—allocating a certain amount of money for vacations, while still prioritizing savings.

It's also important to recognize that compromise may not mean "meeting in the middle" every time. It could mean giving one partner the space to enjoy certain financial luxuries while the other focuses on long-term goals, but with mutual understanding and agreement.

Financial Therapy: A Tool for Healing

If money-related conflicts become too overwhelming or persistent, seeking the help of a financial therapist or counselor can be a productive step. A financial therapist specializes in the emotional aspects of money, helping individuals and couples navigate their financial behaviors and attitudes. Through therapy, couples can better understand their relationship with money and work through financial disagreements in a healthy, productive way.

Financial therapy can also help individuals and couples develop better coping mechanisms for dealing with financial stress, guilt, and anxiety, creating a foundation for healthier financial decisions and stronger relationships.

Conclusion: Building a Stronger, Healthier Financial Partnership

Money has a profound influence on relationships, but it doesn't have to be a source of conflict. By understanding the psychological dynamics of money in relationships, couples can work together to create a healthy financial partnership based on trust, communication, and shared goals. The key is to foster open, honest conversations about money, set clear financial boundaries, and practice mutual respect for each other's financial preferences.

By addressing money issues proactively, couples can strengthen their bond and create a sense of financial security that benefits both partners. As you move forward in your relationship, remember that money doesn't have to divide you—it can be a tool for growth, unity, and shared success.

Chapter 10: The Delayed Gratification Approach

In a world that constantly emphasizes instant rewards, from fast food to one-click shopping and immediate access to entertainment, the ability to delay gratification has become a crucial yet often overlooked skill. Delayed gratification is the practice of resisting the urge to immediately indulge in a reward or pleasure in favor of a larger, long-term benefit. It requires self-discipline, patience, and the foresight to understand that the satisfaction gained from waiting for something is often greater than the fleeting pleasure of immediate consumption.

This chapter explores the concept of delayed gratification, its psychological and emotional benefits, and how it can be applied to personal finance. We will discuss how delayed gratification can help you achieve long-term financial goals, improve decision-making, and enhance overall well-being. By the end of this chapter, you will have a clear understanding of how practicing delayed gratification can be a game-changer in your financial life, helping you avoid impulsive spending and stay focused on your long-term objectives.

What is Delayed Gratification?

Delayed gratification is the ability to resist the temptation for an immediate reward in favor of a later, more substantial reward. It involves self-control and the willingness to wait for a better outcome, even if the immediate reward feels more enticing.

One of the most famous psychological studies on delayed gratification is the "Marshmallow Experiment," conducted by psychologist Walter Mischel in the 1960s. In the experiment, children were given a choice: they could eat one marshmallow immediately, or they could wait 15 minutes and receive two marshmallows instead. The study found that the children who were able to wait and resist the immediate temptation generally performed better later in life, in areas such as academic success and personal health.

This experiment demonstrates the power of delayed gratification—not just in resisting a simple treat, but in the larger context of life, where our ability to delay immediate pleasure can lead to greater success and fulfillment over time.

The Psychology Behind Delayed Gratification

The ability to delay gratification is rooted in our brain's reward system, which is responsible for processing rewards and motivating behavior. When we make a purchase or engage in a pleasurable activity, our brain releases dopamine—the neurotransmitter responsible for feelings of pleasure and satisfaction. However, the brain also has a capacity for self-regulation. Delayed gratification involves controlling the impulsive, dopamine-driven responses that urge us to act immediately, and instead, engaging the part of our brain responsible for long-term planning and goal-setting.

Several factors influence our ability to delay gratification, including:

1. Impulse Control and Emotional Regulation

Self-control is key to delayed gratification. The ability to resist an immediate reward requires controlling impulsive desires, which are often triggered by emotions such as stress, anxiety, or boredom. When we are feeling emotionally vulnerable, we are more likely to seek out quick rewards, such as shopping, eating comfort food, or indulging in a treat. Developing emotional regulation skills—such as mindfulness, deep breathing, or journaling—can help us manage the emotional triggers that lead to impulsive decisions.

2. Future-Oriented Thinking

Delayed gratification also requires a shift in mindset—from focusing on the immediate present to thinking about future rewards. People who practice delayed gratification tend to be more future-oriented, meaning they are able to visualize and plan for long-term goals, such as buying a home, building an emergency fund, or saving for retirement. They recognize that the short-term sacrifice of not indulging in immediate pleasures is worthwhile because it leads to greater rewards down the road.

3. Willpower and Commitment

Willpower is the mental strength needed to resist temptation and stay focused on a long-term goal. It involves commitment to your values, financial goals, and overall well-being. Willpower can be strengthened over time by practicing delayed gratification in small ways, such as resisting the urge to buy something impulsively or sticking to a budget despite temptations. Research has shown that willpower, like a muscle, can be trained and developed with consistent practice.

The Benefits of Delayed Gratification

Practicing delayed gratification can have profound benefits in both your financial life and your overall well-being. Here are some of the key advantages:

1. Achieving Long-Term Financial Goals

One of the most powerful ways delayed gratification impacts your life is by helping you achieve your long-term financial goals. Whether it's saving for a down payment on a house, building an emergency fund, or preparing for retirement, delayed gratification is essential for success. By choosing to delay immediate indulgences—such as eating out, buying new clothes, or upgrading gadgets—you can prioritize saving and investing for the future.

For example, instead of spending money on impulse buys, you could redirect that money toward paying off debt, building savings, or investing in assets that will appreciate over time. The key is to recognize that sacrificing small, immediate pleasures now can lead to a more secure, fulfilling financial future.

2. Reducing Financial Stress

When you give in to the temptation of spending on impulse, it often results in buyer's remorse or financial strain. By practicing delayed gratification, you allow yourself the opportunity to make more thoughtful, intentional decisions about your money. This leads to reduced financial stress, as you're not constantly worried about overspending or accumulating unnecessary debt. Moreover, by saving and investing consistently, you create a buffer against financial emergencies, further decreasing stress and providing peace of mind.

3. Building a Positive Relationship with Money

Delayed gratification helps foster a healthier, more balanced relationship with money. Rather than viewing money as something to be spent immediately, you begin to see it as a tool for achieving your goals. By resisting the urge for short-term rewards, you develop a sense of financial discipline that empowers you to make decisions based on your values rather than fleeting desires.

This mindset shift encourages long-term thinking, where money becomes a means to create a life you truly want, rather than a tool for momentary satisfaction. As you see the results of your savings, investments, and financial planning, you'll feel more in control of your financial future and more confident in your ability to make smart decisions.

4. Improving Self-Control and Personal Development

The act of delaying gratification can also improve self-control in other areas of life, beyond finances. Whether it's resisting unhealthy food, staying committed to a fitness routine, or avoiding distractions when working toward a personal goal, the ability to delay gratification strengthens your willpower and self-discipline. Over time, you build resilience and the ability to stay focused on long-term objectives, rather than seeking out immediate satisfaction.

This improved self-control has far-reaching implications for personal development. As you practice delaying gratification in various areas of your life, you'll develop better habits, achieve greater success in your goals, and feel more in control of your life and choices.

Practical Strategies for Practicing Delayed Gratification

While delayed gratification can be challenging in a world that constantly encourages immediate rewards, there are several strategies you can implement to help you practice it effectively.

1. Set Clear, Tangible Goals

One of the first steps in practicing delayed gratification is to set clear, measurable financial goals. Whether it's saving for a vacation, paying off credit card debt, or building a retirement fund, having a clear vision of your goals can help you stay focused. When you feel the urge to spend impulsively, remind yourself of your goals and the rewards you'll enjoy once you reach them. Visualizing your future success can make it easier to resist short-term temptations.

2. Use the "24-Hour Rule"

A simple yet effective strategy to combat impulse spending is the "24-hour rule." When you feel the urge to make an unplanned purchase, commit to waiting 24 hours before buying it. During this time, you can evaluate whether the purchase is truly necessary or if it's just an emotional reaction. Often, after a day of reflection, you may find that the desire to make the purchase has faded, and you can allocate your money toward your long-term goals instead.

3. Break Large Goals into Smaller Milestones

Delayed gratification doesn't mean waiting for years to see progress—it's about taking small, consistent steps toward your goals. Breaking large financial goals into smaller, more achievable milestones can make them feel more attainable and motivate you to stay on track. For example, if your goal is to save for a down payment on a house, break it down into monthly savings targets that you can easily measure and track.

Each time you hit a milestone, you'll feel a sense of accomplishment that will reinforce your commitment to delayed gratification.

4. Create a Spending Plan and Stick to It

Having a detailed budget or spending plan is one of the most effective ways to practice delayed gratification. By clearly defining how much you can spend on discretionary items each month, you limit the opportunity for impulsive purchases. Once the allocated money for discretionary spending is gone, you'll need to wait until the next month to indulge, which encourages thoughtful decision-making about what's truly worth your money.

5. Practice Mindfulness and Self-Reflection

Mindfulness can help you become more aware of your emotional triggers and the impulses that lead to spontaneous purchases. By practicing mindfulness, you can learn to pause before acting on an urge to spend and reflect on whether the purchase aligns with your goals. Journaling or taking a few moments to ask yourself why you're feeling the urge to buy something can help you gain better control over your spending habits.

Conclusion: The Long-Term Rewards of Delayed Gratification

In a world that celebrates instant gratification, the ability to delay immediate rewards in favor of long-term goals is a powerful tool for achieving financial success and personal growth. By practicing delayed gratification, you can build a solid foundation for your financial future, reduce stress, and cultivate a deeper sense of control and self-discipline.

While it may be challenging at first, the rewards of delayed gratification far outweigh the temporary pleasure of an impulse purchase. By focusing on your long-term goals, making thoughtful spending decisions, and developing a mindset that values patience and planning, you can set yourself on the path to lasting financial well-being and fulfillment.

Chapter 11: Proven Strategies for Saving Money

Saving money is a skill—one that many people struggle to master. With so many temptations in our consumer-driven society, it's easy to fall into the habit of spending impulsively, putting our long-term savings goals on the back burner. However, learning how to save effectively is one of the most important financial habits you can develop. Whether you're saving for an emergency fund, a vacation, retirement, or a big purchase, having a solid savings plan gives you financial security, peace of mind, and the ability to pursue your goals without constantly worrying about money.

In this chapter, we will explore proven strategies for saving money, ranging from simple, everyday changes to more advanced techniques that can help you grow your savings steadily and consistently. Whether you're just starting out or looking to refine your existing saving habits, these strategies can help you build a strong financial foundation for the future.

---

1. Start with a Budget: The Foundation of Saving

The first and most crucial step to saving money is creating a budget. A budget serves as a roadmap for your finances, outlining where your money is coming from and where it's going. Without a budget, it's easy to lose track of spending, and you might find that at the end of the month, there's little or nothing left to save.

How to Create a Budget

- **Track Your Income**: Start by listing all sources of income, including your salary, side jobs, or passive income streams.

- **List Your Expenses**: Break your expenses into two categories: fixed expenses (e.g., rent, utilities, car payments) and variable expenses (e.g., groceries, entertainment, dining out).

- **Set Realistic Savings Goals**: Based on your income and expenses, determine how much you can realistically save each month. Start small and gradually increase your savings goal over time as you identify areas where you can cut back.

- **Use the 50/30/20 Rule**: This rule divides your income into three categories:

    - **50%** for needs (housing, utilities, groceries, insurance)

    - **30%** for wants (entertainment, dining out, shopping)

    - **20%** for savings (emergency fund, retirement, investments)

By tracking your income and expenses, and adhering to a budgeting plan like the 50/30/20 rule, you'll have a clear picture of where your money is going and how much you can allocate toward savings each month.

---

2. Pay Yourself First: Prioritize Savings

One of the most effective ways to ensure you save regularly is to treat savings as a non-negotiable expense. Rather than saving what's left over after spending, "pay yourself first" by setting aside money for savings before you do anything else.

How to Pay Yourself First

- **Automatic Transfers**: Set up an automatic transfer from your checking account to your savings account as soon as you receive your paycheck. This ensures that you save consistently, without the temptation to spend the money.
- **Direct Deposit**: If your employer offers direct deposit, consider having a portion of your paycheck directly deposited into a savings or investment account. This minimizes the chances of spending money before saving it.
- **Save a Fixed Percentage**: Decide on a fixed percentage of your income that you want to save (e.g., 10% or 20%) and make it a non-negotiable part of your financial routine.

By prioritizing savings and setting up automatic transfers, you ensure that saving becomes an automatic, non-discretionary part of your financial life.

---

3. Build an Emergency Fund: Your Safety Net

One of the most important savings goals you can set is building an emergency fund. An emergency fund is a savings buffer that helps you cover unexpected expenses—such as medical bills, car repairs, or job loss—without going into debt.

How to Build an Emergency Fund

- **Set a Goal**: Aim for at least three to six months' worth of living expenses in your emergency fund. This amount will provide enough financial cushion to help you weather most unexpected situations.

- **Start Small**: If saving three to six months of expenses feels overwhelming, start by setting aside a smaller, more attainable goal, such as $500 or $1,000. Once you reach that milestone, build toward a larger fund.

- **Use a Separate Account**: Open a separate savings account for your emergency fund. This makes it less tempting to dip into the fund for non-emergency expenses.

- **Build Gradually**: Rather than attempting to save a large sum all at once, set aside a fixed amount each month. Even small contributions will add up over time.

Having an emergency fund provides peace of mind and prevents you from relying on credit cards or loans when unexpected expenses arise.

---

4. Cut Back on Unnecessary Spending

One of the most direct ways to boost your savings is by cutting back on unnecessary spending. Many of us unknowingly waste money on things we don't truly need, whether it's expensive subscriptions, takeout meals, or impulse purchases.

How to Cut Back on Spending

- **Track Subscriptions**: Many of us are subscribed to services (magazines, streaming platforms, gym memberships) we rarely use. Track these subscriptions and cancel the ones you don't need.

- **Limit Dining Out**: Eating out at restaurants can quickly add up. Consider preparing meals at home or cutting back on dining out a few times a week. You'll save money and likely eat healthier.

- **Impulse Control**: Avoid impulse buys by implementing a waiting period. If you see something you want, wait 24 to 48 hours before making the purchase. This often allows the initial desire to fade and helps you realize that you don't need the item.
- **Shop Smart**: Look for sales, use coupons, or buy generic brands when possible. You don't need to sacrifice quality to save money, but being more strategic with your purchases can make a big difference.

By scrutinizing your expenses and cutting back on non-essential items, you can free up more money to put toward your savings goals.

---

5. Save Windfalls and Bonuses

Windfalls—unexpected sums of money, such as tax refunds, work bonuses, gifts, or inheritance—offer a great opportunity to supercharge your savings. While it's tempting to spend these unexpected funds on fun or luxury purchases, using them to boost your savings can have a lasting impact on your financial future.

How to Save Windfalls

- **Allocate a Portion to Savings**: Rather than spending all of your windfall, commit to putting a percentage (e.g., 50% or 100%) of it directly into your savings account.

- **Use for Specific Goals**: Consider using windfalls to fund specific savings goals, such as a vacation fund, home down payment, or retirement savings.
- **Avoid Lifestyle Inflation**: Resist the urge to increase your spending just because you received extra money. Instead, use the windfall to make long-term financial progress.

By saving windfalls rather than spending them, you can significantly accelerate the growth of your savings and investment accounts.

---

6. Take Advantage of Employer Retirement Plans

If your employer offers a retirement savings plan—such as a 401(k)—it's wise to take full advantage of it. Contributing to your retirement plan not only helps you save for the future but may also come with employer matching contributions, which is essentially "free money."

How to Maximize Retirement Savings

- **Contribute the Maximum Match**: At the very least, contribute enough to take full advantage of your employer's match. For example, if your employer offers a 100% match on the first 5% of your salary, make sure you're contributing that amount to receive the full match.
- **Increase Contributions Over Time**: Once you've hit the match threshold, try to increase your contribution over time. Even small increases can make a big difference over the long term due to compound growth.
- **Consider Other Accounts**: If your employer doesn't offer a retirement plan or you've already maxed out your 401(k), consider contributing to an individual retirement account (IRA) or a Roth IRA to further boost your savings.

By taking advantage of employer retirement plans and maximizing contributions, you can build a secure financial future for your retirement.

---

7. Automate Your Savings

Automation is one of the easiest ways to save money without having to think about it. By setting up automatic transfers to your savings or investment accounts, you make saving a non-negotiable part of your financial routine.

How to Automate Your Savings

- **Set Up Recurring Transfers**: Set up automatic transfers from your checking account to your savings account. These transfers can be scheduled for payday, ensuring that you save before you have the chance to spend.

- **Automate Bill Payments**: Automating your bill payments ensures that you never miss a due date and avoids late fees, which can eat into your savings.

- **Round Up Purchases**: Some apps allow you to round up your purchases to the nearest dollar and deposit the difference into a savings account. While small, this can add up over time.

Automation makes saving effortless and ensures you stick to your financial goals, even if you're busy or forgetful.

Conclusion: Consistency is Key

Saving money is not about making drastic sacrifices or trying to accumulate wealth overnight. It's about developing consistent habits that allow you to gradually build wealth and achieve your financial goals. By following proven strategies like creating a budget, prioritizing savings, building an emergency fund, and automating your savings, you can take control of your financial future and secure long-term stability.

Remember that every little bit counts. Whether it's cutting back on unnecessary spending, saving windfalls, or contributing regularly to retirement plans, small, consistent actions can lead to big results. The key is to make saving a habit and commit to a process of steady growth—over time, your financial picture will improve, bringing you greater peace of mind and the ability to achieve your goals.

Chapter 12: Overcoming Financial Traps

In our quest for financial stability and freedom, it's easy to fall into financial traps—unseen pitfalls that often lead us down a path of debt, stress, and regret. These traps aren't always obvious at first, and they often feel like shortcuts to achieving immediate financial satisfaction. However, in the long run, they can jeopardize our financial health and prevent us from reaching our true financial goals.

This chapter will explore the most common financial traps, how they work, and, most importantly, how to overcome them. From the allure of easy credit to the pressures of lifestyle inflation, we'll break down the psychological forces behind these traps and provide actionable strategies to avoid them. With the right awareness and tools, you can build a financial life that is not only free from these traps but also one that fosters long-term financial health and peace of mind.

---

1. The Debt Trap: The Struggle with Credit and Borrowing

Debt is often the first financial trap people fall into, and it can feel inescapable once you've accumulated credit card balances, loans, or other forms of debt. The temptation of easy credit—such as credit cards, payday loans, or financing options—can lure us into spending beyond our means. While credit can be a helpful tool for managing large expenses or emergencies, when misused, it can quickly lead to a cycle of debt that is difficult to break free from.

How the Debt Trap Works

Credit cards, personal loans, and other borrowing options provide the immediate gratification of purchasing something now and paying for it later. The problem is that many people only focus on the initial payments and ignore the long-term costs of borrowing, such as interest rates, fees, and debt accumulation. This can result in a situation where the total amount owed becomes far larger than the original purchase price, leading to ongoing stress and financial instability.

Furthermore, once you're in debt, it can be difficult to escape. As you make monthly payments, interest accrues, and it often feels like you're barely making a dent in your debt. For many, the burden of debt becomes overwhelming, leading to more borrowing just to stay afloat.

How to Overcome the Debt Trap

- **Pay Off High-Interest Debt First**: Prioritize paying off high-interest debt, such as credit cards, before focusing on other financial goals. The longer you carry high-interest debt, the more you'll end up paying in the long run. Consider the debt snowball or debt avalanche methods to aggressively tackle what you owe.

- **Stop Using Credit Cards**: If you're struggling with debt, consider pausing credit card use until you're back on track. This will prevent further purchases and interest charges from accumulating.

- **Create a Debt Repayment Plan**: Set a clear plan for paying off your debt and stick to it. Break down the total amount you owe into manageable payments, and avoid taking on new debt during this time.

- **Use Cash or Debit**: When possible, pay with cash or a debit card to avoid the temptation of credit. This forces you to live within your means and prevents accumulating more debt.

The key to overcoming the debt trap is a commitment to paying it down, living within your means, and creating a plan to avoid future debt.

---

2. The Lifestyle Inflation Trap: Keeping Up with the Joneses

As our income increases, it's easy to succumb to the allure of upgrading our lifestyle. The extra income is often seen as an opportunity to spend more—buying a nicer car, moving to a bigger house, or indulging in luxury experiences. While it's tempting to enjoy the fruits of your labor, lifestyle inflation can quickly consume any financial progress you've made, leaving you with less savings and more stress.

How the Lifestyle Inflation Trap Works

Lifestyle inflation occurs when your spending increases as your income increases. At first, it seems harmless–a nicer apartment, a more expensive wardrobe, or upgrading to a newer car. However, these "upgrades" often come with higher monthly expenses, leaving little room for savings or investing. Over time, what started as a modest increase in spending can snowball, making it difficult to save for long-term goals such as retirement, homeownership, or financial independence.

The trap lies in the mindset shift that occurs: as your income grows, your expenses grow in parallel, and the feeling of never having enough money persists. You become accustomed to a higher standard of living, and the thought of downsizing or cutting back becomes unappealing, even though it could greatly improve your financial situation.

How to Overcome the Lifestyle Inflation Trap

- **Save and Invest Before Spending**: Whenever you receive a pay raise or windfall, commit to saving or investing a significant portion before increasing your spending. By prioritizing savings first, you build long-term wealth while still allowing yourself some room for lifestyle upgrades.

- **Live Below Your Means**: Rather than increasing your spending every time your income increases, choose to live below your means. This creates financial flexibility and allows you to accumulate wealth over time. Focus on purchasing only what aligns with your long-term goals, rather than indulging in unnecessary luxuries.

- **Avoid Keeping Up with Others**: Social comparison can make lifestyle inflation more tempting. Resist the urge to compete with friends, family, or colleagues when it comes to material possessions. Remember that what matters most is your financial well-being, not matching others' spending habits.

By consciously choosing not to inflate your lifestyle, you can maintain financial discipline and build a stronger foundation for the future.

---

3. The Instant Gratification Trap: Impulse Purchases and Immediate Rewards

In a world driven by convenience and instant rewards, the desire for immediate satisfaction often leads to impulse purchases. Whether it's grabbing a coffee, buying clothes on sale, or upgrading gadgets, the instant gratification trap can lead to unnecessary spending that sabotages your long-term savings goals.

How the Instant Gratification Trap Works

Instant gratification is the desire to experience pleasure right now, rather than waiting for a better, more lasting reward. This impulse-driven behavior is reinforced by the convenience of online shopping, fast food, and same-day delivery services. In many cases, it's not that you need the item, but rather that you want it in the moment, and the emotional satisfaction of buying it feels good.

However, the problem with instant gratification is that the pleasure is short-lived. Once the excitement of the purchase fades, the item is often relegated to the back of your closet or the bottom of a drawer, leaving you with more stuff and less money. The cycle of chasing fleeting pleasure leads to financial insecurity and stress.

How to Overcome the Instant Gratification Trap

- **Practice Delayed Gratification**: As discussed in Chapter 10, practicing delayed gratification is key to avoiding impulse buys. When you feel the urge to make an impulsive purchase, pause and give yourself time to reflect. Often, waiting 24 hours or more helps diminish the desire to buy something on impulse.

- **Set Spending Limits**: Establish a set amount of money you are willing to spend each month on discretionary purchases, and stick to it. If you hit your limit, avoid making additional purchases for the rest of the month.

- **Mindful Spending**: Before making a purchase, ask yourself whether the item aligns with your long-term goals and values. Will it improve your life or is it simply an emotional reaction to boredom, stress, or social influence? By being more mindful of your spending, you can reduce the impact of impulse buys on your finances.

---

4. The False Sense of Financial Security Trap: Living Paycheck to Paycheck

Even when your income is decent, living paycheck to paycheck can still be a major financial trap. This occurs when you spend everything you earn each month, leaving no room for savings or investments. A false sense of financial security arises because you're comfortable with your current income and lifestyle, but this leaves you vulnerable to financial emergencies and unable to build wealth.

How the False Sense of Financial Security Trap Works

Living paycheck to paycheck often stems from poor financial habits or a lack of awareness about your spending. The idea that you're "getting by" can lead to complacency, making it easy to ignore savings goals or emergency preparedness. Without a safety net, you're one unexpected expense away from financial chaos.

Moreover, the comfort of a regular paycheck can create the illusion that everything is fine, even though you're not building toward long-term financial independence. This lack of savings or investment can prevent you from achieving major financial milestones, like buying a home, traveling, or retiring comfortably.

How to Overcome the False Sense of Financial Security Trap

- **Build an Emergency Fund**: One of the first steps to escaping the paycheck-to-paycheck cycle is to build an emergency fund. Aim to save at least three to six months' worth of living expenses in a separate savings account. This provides a buffer against unexpected expenses like medical bills, car repairs, or job loss.

- **Automate Savings**: Set up automatic transfers to a savings account as soon as you receive your paycheck. This ensures that saving is a priority, not an afterthought.

- **Cut Back on Expenses**: Review your spending and identify areas where you can cut back. Reducing unnecessary expenses—such as subscriptions, dining out, or impulse buys—frees up money to put toward savings and investments.

By building savings and focusing on long-term goals, you can break free from the false sense of financial security and move toward a more stable financial future.

---

5. The "Too Good to Be True" Trap: Scams and High-Risk Investments

Finally, the "too good to be true" trap involves falling for scams, high-risk investments, or get-rich-quick schemes that promise large returns with minimal effort. These opportunities often appeal to our desire for instant wealth and financial freedom, but they can lead to significant financial loss and emotional distress.

How the "Too Good to Be True" Trap Works

Scams and high-risk investments often prey on individuals' lack of financial knowledge or their desperation for quick wealth. Whether it's a high-yield investment that promises astronomical returns or a "too good to be true" business opportunity, these schemes exploit our desire for instant success.

In some cases, individuals fall victim to fraud or deceptive marketing, losing large sums of money or incurring significant debt. Even if the investment doesn't turn out to be fraudulent, the high risks often lead to substantial losses.

How to Overcome the "Too Good to Be True" Trap

- **Be Skeptical of Unrealistic Promises**: If something seems too good to be true, it probably is. Avoid investments or opportunities that promise extraordinary returns with little to no risk.
- **Do Your Research**: Always research any investment or financial opportunity thoroughly. Consult with a financial advisor or seek advice from trusted sources before committing your money.
- **Stick to Proven Strategies**: Invest in established and reliable options, such as retirement accounts, stocks, bonds, and real estate. These investments may take time to grow, but they are far safer and more predictable than high-risk ventures.

By remaining cautious and informed, you can avoid falling for risky schemes and focus on building wealth through sound, proven financial strategies.

Conclusion: Escaping the Financial Traps

Financial traps are a part of modern life, but with awareness and discipline, you can avoid them. Whether it's the debt trap, lifestyle inflation, instant gratification, or the lure of "too good to be true" opportunities, recognizing these pitfalls is the first step toward financial freedom. By creating a solid financial plan, prioritizing saving, and making intentional spending decisions, you can protect yourself from these traps and build a stable, secure financial future.

Chapter 13: The Psychology Behind Every Purchase: What, Why, When & How We Spend – Master Habits, Outsmart Traps, and Take Control of Your Money

Spending money is a routine part of life, but the reasons behind why we spend, how we make financial decisions, and when we're most likely to splurge often go unnoticed. In fact, many of our spending habits are deeply rooted in psychology and behavior patterns that we don't consciously acknowledge. This chapter will break down the *What,*

Why, *When*, and *How* of the psychology of spending, offering readers the understanding and tools necessary to master their money habits and avoid falling into common financial traps.

By understanding the intricate psychological forces behind our spending decisions, we can develop more thoughtful, intentional financial habits that align with our long-term goals. Rather than reacting impulsively to our emotions, social influences, or marketing tactics, we can take control of our money and use it in a way that serves our best interests.

What is the Psychology of Spending?

Spending money is not a purely rational or transactional activity; it is influenced by a range of psychological and emotional factors. We often think of spending as a simple exchange: we give money in return for goods or services. However, the psychology of spending delves deeper, focusing on the underlying reasons behind our choices to purchase.

The *What* of spending involves understanding that our purchasing decisions are often driven by emotional impulses, social pressures, and unconscious biases rather than purely practical needs. These psychological forces influence not only our purchasing habits but also how we feel about money, our financial goals, and our relationship with material goods.

Key Aspects of the Psychology of Spending:

- **Emotional Spending**: Many of our purchases are driven by emotions such as boredom, stress, sadness, or even happiness. Retail therapy, for instance, is a common behavior in which people buy things to fill emotional gaps.

- **Cognitive Biases**: Cognitive biases like anchoring (the tendency to rely too heavily on the first piece of information we encounter), loss aversion (the fear of losing something we already have), and the scarcity effect (the tendency to value something more if it's perceived as limited) often shape our buying behavior.

- **Social Influence**: Social factors such as peer pressure, cultural norms, and the desire to fit in can significantly affect our spending habits. The fear of missing out (FOMO) and the desire to keep up with others can lead us to purchase things we don't need.

Understanding the *What* behind spending helps us recognize that it's not just about the transaction; it's about what triggers us to make purchases and how those triggers affect our financial well-being.

Why Do We Spend?

The *Why* of spending is an essential aspect of understanding how our financial habits are formed. People spend for many different reasons, but most of those reasons are not always tied to necessity or rational thought. Let's explore some of the most common reasons behind why we spend money.

1. Emotional Fulfillment

Emotional spending is one of the most powerful motivators of purchasing behavior. When we feel stressed, anxious, or sad, we may turn to spending money as a way to temporarily ease those negative emotions. It's a form of emotional relief or distraction—a quick way to boost our mood or self-esteem. Whether it's buying a new dress, grabbing takeout, or splurging on a new gadget, emotional purchases are often driven by the need for comfort, validation, or immediate pleasure.

- **Coping with Stress**: Studies show that people often shop to relieve stress or negative emotions. Buying something new offers a temporary emotional boost, but this can create a cycle of buying to manage emotions without truly solving the underlying issue.

- **Filling a Void**: Some individuals spend money to fill an emotional void or to compensate for feelings of inadequacy. The act of purchasing something can temporarily make us feel good about ourselves, but the satisfaction is fleeting, leaving behind feelings of regret.

2. Social Pressure and Comparison

Social pressures, including cultural norms, societal expectations, and peer influence, can significantly affect how we spend. The need to conform to a certain lifestyle, keep up with friends, or project a certain image can lead us to make purchases that aren't aligned with our true needs or financial goals.

- **Social Media and FOMO**: Platforms like Instagram and Facebook often showcase curated images of an idealized lifestyle, leading to social comparison. We may feel the pressure to buy products or experiences to fit in or appear successful, even if they don't align with our financial capabilities.

- **Keeping Up with the Joneses**: People often feel compelled to spend money on things that others in their social circles own or do. Whether it's upgrading a car, buying a new phone, or taking expensive vacations, we may make purchases based on social influence rather than personal need.

3. Desire for Instant Gratification

Human beings are wired for instant gratification—the desire to experience pleasure immediately, rather than delaying satisfaction for a future reward. In a world where instant access to products and services is just a click away, it's easy to give in to the temptation of immediate rewards. When we purchase something, the rush of dopamine that our brains release creates a pleasurable feeling, reinforcing the urge to spend more.

- **Instant Pleasure vs. Long-Term Gain**: The desire for instant pleasure can override long-term financial goals. We may choose to spend on a new luxury item rather than saving for a retirement fund or an emergency fund because the immediate reward feels more satisfying in the moment.

- **The Ease of Online Shopping**: The advent of online shopping has made it easier than ever to indulge in instant gratification. With fast delivery services and easy access to credit, buying things online has become a seamless experience, leading us to make purchases without much thought.

4. Lack of Financial Awareness

Many of us spend without fully understanding the long-term consequences of our actions. Without a clear understanding of personal finance, people often make purchases based on the desire for immediate satisfaction rather than considering how those purchases will affect their future.

- **Living Paycheck to Paycheck**: A lack of financial education often results in individuals living paycheck to paycheck. When there is no clear financial plan or budget, it becomes easy to spend without tracking how much is being spent or how much should be saved.

- **Impulse Buying**: Without a structured approach to budgeting, impulse buys become more frequent. Without a plan, it's easy to succumb to the urge to buy things that aren't essential, which can derail long-term savings and investment goals.

When Do We Spend?

Understanding when we are most susceptible to spending is crucial for taking control of our financial decisions. There are certain times and emotional states when we are more likely to make poor financial decisions or fall prey to impulse buying.

1. When We're Emotional

Emotional triggers, such as stress, anxiety, sadness, or even extreme happiness, can influence our spending habits. When we are feeling vulnerable or overwhelmed, we may turn to shopping as a way to cope with our emotions. This is why retail therapy is so popular—people use spending as a way to alleviate negative emotions or enhance positive ones.

- **Stress Relief**: Many people shop as a way to deal with stress or pressure. When feeling stressed, the act of buying something new can temporarily take the edge off, but it doesn't solve the underlying emotional issues.

- **Rewarding Ourselves**: People often spend money to reward themselves after accomplishing a task, achieving a goal, or simply to celebrate a positive event. However, these rewards often feel unsatisfying in the long run, especially if the purchase wasn't truly necessary.

2. During Sales or Special Promotions

Sales and promotions are designed to trigger a sense of urgency in consumers. The feeling that a "deal" is too good to miss pushes us into making purchases we might not need. Limited-time offers, seasonal sales, and discounts often create a sense of scarcity and urgency, leading us to act quickly, often without fully considering whether we actually need the item.

- **Fear of Missing Out (FOMO)**: The pressure to act quickly before a sale ends or an item sells out can lead to impulse purchases. The fear of missing a good deal is one of the biggest psychological triggers in marketing.

3. Social Events or Holidays

Holidays, birthdays, and other special events often trigger increased spending. These occasions are often marked by a desire to give gifts, celebrate, and share experiences with others. The pressure to buy gifts or participate in group activities can lead to overspending, especially if it's done out of social obligation rather than personal desire.

- **Holiday Spending**: During the holiday season, people tend to spend more on gifts and entertainment. The pressure to buy the "perfect" gift or have the "best" holiday experience often leads to overspending.

How We Spend: The Psychological Triggers and the Power of Marketing

The *How* of spending is often determined by external influences, particularly marketing and advertising. Marketers are experts in understanding consumer psychology and use various strategies to influence our purchasing decisions. Whether it's through the scarcity effect, social proof, or emotional appeals, marketers know how to trigger spending behaviors that feel irresistible.

1. Marketing Tactics

Marketers use specific techniques to play on our psychological tendencies:

- **Scarcity**: Creating a sense of urgency by framing a product as limited in quantity or availability.
- **Social Proof**: Using testimonials, influencer endorsements, and customer reviews to make us believe that a product is popular or desirable.
- **Anchoring**: Providing a reference point (e.g., "original price $100, now $50") to make a deal seem more attractive than it actually is.

2. Consumer Habits and Patterns

Over time, spending habits become ingrained in our daily routines. These habits often form unconsciously, but once established, they can be difficult to break. By understanding how consumer habits are developed and recognizing when they are formed, we can begin to take steps to adjust our spending behaviors for the better.

Conclusion: Mastering the Psychology of Spending

Understanding the *What, Why, When, and How* of spending is the key to mastering your money habits and avoiding financial traps. By recognizing the emotional, social, and psychological forces behind your financial decisions, you can make more conscious, deliberate choices that align with your long-term goals.

To break free from unhealthy spending patterns, focus on developing mindfulness in your financial decisions, practicing delayed gratification, and aligning your spending with your values and priorities. By being intentional about when and why you spend, you can regain control over your finances, build lasting wealth, and achieve the financial freedom you desire.

Mastering the psychology of spending doesn't mean depriving yourself of life's pleasures—it means becoming more aware of your financial behaviors and ensuring that your spending decisions are intentional, thoughtful, and aligned with your goals. Take control of your money today and start making smarter financial decisions that will benefit you in the long run.

Conclusion: Mastering Your Money and Achieving Financial Freedom

Throughout this book, we've explored the complex and powerful relationship between psychology and money—how emotions, cultural influences, and mental patterns can shape our spending decisions and financial behavior. From the psychology of spending to the impact of marketing, the role of fear and scarcity, and the influence of consumerism on our identity, we've uncovered the many ways that our financial choices are influenced by forces both within and beyond our control.

But the key takeaway from this journey is this: **you have the power to take control of your financial destiny**. The behaviors that lead to financial struggles–impulsive spending, living paycheck to paycheck, falling into debt–are not fixed or inevitable. By understanding the psychology behind these behaviors and employing the proven strategies we've discussed, you can break free from the cycles that hold you back and start making conscious, intentional financial decisions.

Empowerment Through Awareness

The first step toward financial freedom is awareness. Simply understanding how our emotions, societal pressures, and subconscious biases influence our spending habits can give us the power to make different choices. You now know how marketing and advertising prey on our desire for instant gratification and how consumerism can erode our sense of self-worth by tying our identity to material possessions.

You've learned that financial success is not about earning more money, but about **how you manage and save the money you already have**. Through strategies like budgeting, paying yourself first, and prioritizing savings, you can lay the foundation for long-term financial security. And by practicing delayed gratification and avoiding the traps of lifestyle inflation, impulse spending, and debt, you can build wealth steadily over time.

Building a Strong Financial Future

It's not just about avoiding traps; it's also about setting yourself up for success. Building an emergency fund, saving for retirement, and investing wisely are all critical components of a secure financial future. But these goals can't be achieved by simply going through the motions. They require **commitment, discipline, and patience**—the ability to delay immediate gratification for long-term rewards.

As you move forward, remember that building wealth is a marathon, not a sprint. Small, consistent actions—whether it's setting aside a portion of your income for savings, cutting back on unnecessary expenses, or investing for the future—will compound over time to create lasting financial freedom.

The Power of Financial Discipline and Emotional Control

The final piece of the puzzle is emotional control. Throughout this book, we've discussed how emotional spending and poor financial habits often stem from **emotional triggers**—stress, boredom, fear, and even social pressures. By understanding these triggers and developing healthier coping mechanisms, you can break free from the cycle of emotional spending and take a more disciplined approach to your money.

Whether it's practicing mindfulness, setting clear financial goals, or seeking professional guidance through financial therapy, emotional awareness is key to developing a **healthier, more balanced relationship with money**. By recognizing when you're acting on impulse and learning to resist those urges, you can make smarter financial decisions that align with your true values and long-term objectives.

Final Thoughts: Taking Charge of Your Financial Journey

The journey toward financial freedom is one of self-awareness, growth, and change. It's about more than just saving money or investing wisely; it's about cultivating the mindset and habits that will support your financial goals. **You are in control** of your money, and with the right knowledge and strategies, you can unlock the doors to a secure, prosperous future.

By applying the principles outlined in this book, you can develop a **financially empowered mindset**—one that values patience, discipline, and intentionality. Over time, you'll not only achieve your financial goals but also experience the peace of mind that comes with knowing you are in control of your financial destiny.

Remember, **financial freedom isn't just about accumulating wealth—it's about creating a life where your financial decisions align with your deepest values and goals**. Whether you're working toward a debt-free life, saving for a dream vacation, or building wealth for retirement, the strategies in this book will guide you every step of the way.

You have everything you need to create a healthier relationship with money and build a secure financial future. The time to start is now. Let go of the habits that have held you back, embrace the new strategies you've learned, and step confidently into your financial future.

Your journey to financial freedom starts today.

For Spending: Start with "**WHY**" and "**HOW**"
For Requirement: Start with "**WHAT**" and "**WHEN**"

ABOUT THE AUTHOR

S S Dhar (Sujit Sutradhar)

📚 Author | Visionary Thinker | Founder of PingShopping.com

🌐 ssdhar.com | pingshopping.com

S S Dhar, born in 1998, is not just an author—he is a force of introspection, insight, and innovation. A passionate educator and a fearless writer, he has dedicated his life to exploring the deeper truths of human existence while empowering others through words that provoke, inspire, and transform.

With a Bachelor of Science completed in 2019 and a brief stint at a prestigious Central University for a Master's in Mathematics, his academic journey took an unconventional turn. At just 17, Dhar's literary consciousness ignited—fueled by poetry, self-help, business insights, and the psychology of success. His writing bridges the practical with the philosophical, transforming complex ideas into compelling narratives. Each book is not just a read—it's a revelation.

Now in his late twenties, S S Dhar has authored over 10 impactful books spanning genres such as personal growth, entrepreneurship, literature, and human potential. His works have sold tens of thousands of copies globally, earning him a place among thought leaders who write to challenge, not conform.

But his journey doesn't stop with books. He is the Founder of PingShopping.com—a rapidly growing digital platform dedicated to helping people live healthier, wealthier, smarter, and more balanced lives. Through expertly curated content and valuable products. Join the smarter living movement at: pingshopping.com

With a clear mission—to enrich lives with truth, clarity, and practical wisdom—S S Dhar continues to inspire a new generation of curious minds, thinkers, and dreamers. His words are not merely read; they are remembered. If you're seeking bold ideas, fresh perspectives, and deeply human stories crafted with care and purpose, you've just found your next favor.ite author. Explore his work at: ssdhar.com

www.ingramcontent.com/pod-product-compliance
Lightning Source LLC
Chambersburg PA
CBHW062139160726
48282CB00027B/872
* 9 7 8 9 3 3 4 3 4 0 2 1 1 *